Real-Time Twilio and Flybase

Build Real-Time Web Apps Using Twilio and Flybase with Node.js

Roger Stringer

Apress®

Real-Time Twilio and Flybase: Build Real-Time Web Apps Using Twilio and Flybase with Node.js

Roger Stringer
Penticton, BC, Canada

ISBN-13 (pbk): 978-1-4842-7073-8   ISBN-13 (electronic): 978-1-4842-7074-5
https://doi.org/10.1007/978-1-4842-7074-5

Managing Director, Apress Media LLC: Welmoed Spahr
Acquisitions Editor: Louise Corrigan
Development Editor: James Markham
Coordinating Editor: Jessica Vakili

Cover designed by eStudioCalamar

Cover image designed by Freepik (www.freepik.com)

Distributed to the book trade worldwide by Springer Science+Business Media New York, 1 New York Plaza, New York, NY 10004. Phone 1-800-SPRINGER, fax (201) 348-4505, e-mail orders-ny@springer-sbm.com, or visit www.springeronline.com. Apress Media, LLC is a California LLC and the sole member (owner) is Springer Science + Business Media Finance Inc (SSBM Finance Inc). SSBM Finance Inc is a **Delaware** corporation.

For information on translations, please e-mail booktranslations@springernature.com; for reprint, paperback, or audio rights, please e-mail bookpermissions@springernature.com.

Apress titles may be purchased in bulk for academic, corporate, or promotional use. eBook versions and licenses are also available for most titles. For more information, reference our Print and eBook Bulk Sales web page at http://www.apress.com/bulk-sales.

Any source code or other supplementary material referenced by the author in this book is available to readers on GitHub via the book's product page, located at www.apress.com/9781484270738. For more detailed information, please visit http://www.apress.com/source-code.

Printed on acid-free paper

To my daughter Kaitlyn

Table of Contents

About the Author

Roger Stringer is the founder of Flybase, a real-time application platform that makes it easy for developers to design, build, and scale real-time web and mobile apps in minutes instead of days using client-side code. You can find him on Twitter @freekrai.

About the Technical Reviewer

Rami Morrar is a self-taught programmer and has coding experience in languages such as C# and C++ for over three years. He has made different coding projects, such as a gaming tutorial website, several desktop applications, and even games in the Unity game engine. He is currently working on his own independent game project in MonoGame, set to be released next year. He has an abundance of charisma for programming and gamedev and talks about them on his blog/made tutorials on the MonoGame framework. He is also cowriting a sequel to the book *MonoGame Mastery*. In his free time, he likes to play games and look at cool new projects by other indie developers.

Introduction

This book is a collection of a series of previously published blog posts showcasing how to use Twilio and Flybase together to build real-time apps, as well as some new never-before-seen content.

For some background, my name is Roger Stringer. I'm the founder of and lead developer for `https://flybase.io`, as well as the author of *Twilio Cookbook* (first and second editions). I've worked with Twilio's API for several years and have been building Flybase (and apps with Flybase) for over three years.

`https://flybase.io` is a web platform used to store and retrieve data in real time, as well as to send and receive real-time events such as triggers for incoming calls, incoming messages, agents logging off, etc. These two services make a truly winning combination for gathering real-time data, so I wanted to present them here together in this book.

What This Book Covers

Chapter 1, "Building a Real-Time SMS Call Center": Learn to use Twilio and Flybase and send and receive SMS messages from a browser and see them in real time.

Chapter 2, "Building a Live Blogging Tool": Use Twilio and Flybase to build a real-time live blogging tool where users can send text messages and media and have them appear on a web page for readers to read.

Chapter 3, "Building a Real-Time Group Chat App": Build a group chat app to send messages to multiple group members, handy for events.

Chapter 4, "Creating a Click-to-Call Call Center": Build a "click-to-call" call center, where users can click a link on a web page and initiate a browser-to-browser phone call using Flybase and Twilio Client with a live agent.

Chapter 5, "Building a Salesforce-Powered Call Center": Build a Salesforce (or any CRM)-embeddable call center or automated call distribution (ACD).

Chapter 6, "Sending Daily SMS Reminders": Send daily automated SMS messages to users for multipurpose marketing/advertising opportunities.

Chapter 7, "Building a Real-Time Call Tracking Dashboard": Learn how to build a real-time call tracking dashboard to track where incoming calls are coming from.

CHAPTER 1

Building a Real-Time SMS Call Center

We're going to build a handy SMS call center for our first project.

This call center will handle incoming SMS messages from users; it won't handle voice, just SMS. We'll look at voice in a couple other chapters.

Do you want to know one of the beautiful things about Flybase? It integrates really easily with other services.

In this chapter, we are going to walk through using Flybase and Twilio together to build a real-time SMS call center.

This could be used as a customer help desk where customers send a text message for help and an agent sends a reply back from their web browser.

The actual phone work will be handled by Twilio, and Flybase will store the data and display the chats in real time. We'll use Node.js to send and receive the text messages and an HTML frontend to handle the actual chatting.

The Setup

We'll be using a few tools to build this app. You'll want to have these set up before you continue on:

- Twilio (http://twilio.com): To send and receive SMS messages. Don't have a Twilio account? Sign up for free (www.twilio.com/try-twilio).

© Roger Stringer 2021
R. Stringer, *Real-Time Twilio and Flybase*, https://doi.org/10.1007/978-1-4842-7074-5_1

- Flybase (`www.flybase.io/`): A real-time database API. We'll be using it to store our incoming and outgoing messages.

- Node.js (`http://nodejs.org/`): A platform built on Chrome's JavaScript runtime for easily building fast, scalable network applications.

If you haven't already, sign up (`https://app.flybase.io/signup`) for a free Flybase account now and then create a new app. You'll use your app for your call center.

Getting Started

We first need to set up our **Node.js** app.

Besides the Twilio and Flybase modules, we'll be using the Express framework (`http://expressjs.com/`) to set up our node web server to receive the POST request from Twilio, so we'll need to install the express package. We'll also be using the body-parser module, so we are going to install that as well.

Let's create our `package.json` file:

```javascript
{
    "name": "sms-contact-center",
    "version": "0.0.1",
    "description": "SMS Contact Center powered by Flybase,
                    Twilio and Node.js",
    "main": "app.js",
    "repository": "https://github.com/flybase/sms-contact",
    "scripts": {
            "test": "echo \"Error: no test specified\" && exit 1"
    },
```

```
    "keywords": [
            "twilio",
            "Flybase",
            "sms"
    ],
    "author": "Roger Stringer",
    "license": "MIT",
    "dependencies": {
            "twilio": "~1.6.0",
            "ejs": "~0.8.5",
            "express": "~3.4.8",
            "flybase": "~1.7.8",
            "node-buzz": "~1.1.0",
            "moment": "~2.5.1",
            "less-middleware": "~0.2.1-beta",
            "body-parser" : "~1.4.2",
            "method-override" : "~2.0.2"
    },
    "engines": {
            "node": "0.10.26"
    }
}
```

Save this file, and from the terminal, run the following command:

```javascript
npm install
```

This will create a node_modules folder containing all of the modules we want to use.

Let's set up our folder structure; create a folder called views. This is where we will keep our frontend.

Now, create a folder called "public." This will host our static files. Inside that folder, create a css folder and a js folder; we'll come back to these later.

At the beginning of our app.js file, we'll need to require express and initialize it into a variable called app.

We're also going to use the bodyParser middleware (https://github.com/expressjs/body-parser) to make it easy to use the data we'll be getting in our POST request.

Create a new file called app.js and require the twilio, express, and flybase packages:

```javascript
var express = require('express');
var bodyParser = require('body-parser');
var methodOverride = require('method-override');
var twilio = require('twilio');
var  path = require('path');

var app = express();
app.set('views', path.join(process.cwd(), 'views'));
app.set('view engine', 'ejs');
app.use(bodyParser.json());
app.use(bodyParser.urlencoded({ extended: true }));
app.use(express.static(__dirname + '/public'));

var port = process.env.PORT || 8080; // set our port

var client = twilio('ACCOUNTSID', 'AUTHTOKEN');
var twilio_number = 'YOUR-NUMBER';

var api_key = "YOUR-API-KEY";
var appname = "YOUR-FLYBASE-APP";
```

```
var collection = "smscontact";
var messagesRef = require('flybase').init(appname, collection,
                  api_key);

// backend routes =========================
```

Replace ACCOUNTSID, AUTHTOKEN, and YOUR-NUMBER with your Twilio credentials and a phone number in your Twilio account that you'll be using.

Then, replace YOUR-API-KEY, YOUR-flybase-APP, and smscontact with your Flybase API Key, and create a collection to use. If you haven't already created a collection, one will be automatically created for you when you first save data, so you can leave the collection name set to smscontact if you want.

Flybase uses collections to organize data inside apps, so one app could have several collections. If you're familiar with relational databases, this is the equivalent of a table.

This is the start of our app. Next, we'll tell it what to do when new texts come in and when an agent replies to a text.

Sending and Receiving Texts

Twilio uses webhooks (https://en.wikipedia.org/wiki/Webhook) to let your server know when an incoming message or phone call comes into our app. We need to set up an endpoint that we can tell Twilio to use for the messaging webhook.

We're going to add a route for /message that responds with some TwiML (Twilio Markup Language, www.twilio.com/docs/api/twiml). TwiML is a basic set of instructions you can use to tell Twilio what to do when you receive an incoming call or SMS message. Our code will look like this:

```javascript
app.post('/message', function (request, response) {
    var d = new Date();
    var date = d.toLocaleString();

    messagesRef.push({
        sid: request.param('MessageSid'),
        type:'text',
        direction: "inbound",
        tstamp: date,
        fromNumber:request.param('From'),
        textMessage:request.param('Body'),
        fromCity:request.param('FromCity'),
        fromState:request.param('FromState'),
        fromCountry:request.param('FromCountry')
    });

    var resp = new twilio.TwimlResponse();
    resp.message('Thanks for the message, an agent will get
    back to you shortly.');
    response.writeHead(200, {
        'Content-Type':'text/xml'
    });
    response.end(resp.toString());
});
```

This will listen for any incoming SMS messages and store them inside
your Flybase app.

Once a message has been received, we use the Twilio node library
to initialize a new TwimlResponse. We then use the **message** keyword
(www.twilio.com/docs/api/twiml/sms/message) to set what we want
to respond to the message with. In this case, we'll just say "Thanks
for the message, an agent will get back to you shortly." Then we'll set

the content-type of our response to text/xml and send the string representation of the TwimlResponse we built.

Whenever a customer sends a message to the phone number we've set up, it will send them the response and store the message inside Flybase. If an agent is watching the client, then they will see the message appear instantly and can send a reply back.

Now, let's add a route called /reply. This is what we will call via AJAX when our agents want to reply to a message:

```javascript
app.post('/reply', function (request, response) {
    var d = new Date();
    var date = d.toLocaleString();

    messagesRef.push({
        type:'text',
        direction: "outbound",
        tstamp: date,
        fromNumber:request.param('From'),
        textMessage:request.param('Body'),
        fromCity:'',
        fromState:'',
        fromCountry:''
    });

    client.sendMessage( {
        to:request.param('To'),
        from:twilio_number,
        body:request.param('Body')
    }, function( err, data ) {
        console.log( data.body );
    });
});
```

This will store the reply in our Flybase app as an outbound reply and send the message to the customer.

Finally, let's set our server to listen on port 8080 and tell it what to do when we view it from a browser:

```javascript
// frontend routes ==========================

// route to handle all angular requests
app.get('*', function(req, res) {
    res.render('home', {
        apikey:api_key,
        appname:appname,
        collection:collection
    });
});

var server = app.listen(port, function() {
        console.log('Listening on port %d', server.address().port);
});
```

Now that we've built our server, we need to tell Twilio to use this messaging URL as our Message Request URL.

Send an SMS message to your Twilio number, and you should get a response back. If you don't, take a look at the Twilio App Monitor (www.twilio.com/user/account/developer-tools/app-monitor) to help determine what went wrong.

This is the backend portion of our call center; it listens for incoming text messages, stores them in our Flybase app, and then sends replies when an agent replies.

Now, we need to build our agent system, where an agent can watch incoming messages and reply to them.

We'll build that now.

The Client

We've got our Node.js app listening for messages to send and receive. Now let's set up our client, which is what agents will see from their web browser.

When a message comes in, we'll display a chat box showing the message and then send a reply.

First, let's create our view. In the /views folder, create a file called home.ejs:

HTML
```
<!doctype html>
<html>
<head>
        <link href='http://fonts.googleapis.com/css?family=
        Lato:400,300italic,400italic&subset=latin,latin-ext'
        rel='stylesheet' type='text/css'>
        <link rel="stylesheet" type="text/css" href="http://
        angular-ui.github.com/ng-grid/css/ng-grid.css" />
        <link rel="stylesheet" href="http://maxcdn.bootstrapcdn.
        com/bootstrap/3.2.0/css/bootstrap.min.css">
        <link rel="stylesheet" type="text/css" href="/css/style.
        css">

        <script src="https://ajax.googleapis.com/ajax/libs/
        jquery/1.7.2/jquery.min.js"></script>
        <script src="https://cdn.flybase.io/flybase.
        js?latest=1"></script>
        <script src="/js/chat.js"></script>

        <title>SMS Contact Center, powered by Flybase and
        Twilio</title>
</head>
<body>
```

9

```html
<div class='container'>
    <br />
    <div class="well">
        <p class='homefont'>Welcome to your SMS
        Contact Center</p>

        <p class='homefont'>This call center is the
        start of a modern day call center.</p>

        <p class='homefont'>Take a look around and
        give us a try.</p>
    </div>
    <hr/>
    <h3>Incoming messages</h3>
    <div id="templateContainer"></div>
</div>
<script>
    $(function(){
// initializes our Flybase object
        var flybaseRef = new flybase("<%= apikey %>",
        "<%= appname %>", "<%= collection %>");
// start our chatManager.
        var myChatManager = new chatManager(
        flybaseRef );
        myChatManager.updateChats();
    });
</script>
</body>
</html>
```

This file will act as our HTML file, and we are using EJS so we can pass our Flybase settings and not have to configure them in multiple places. EJS is handy for adding template functionality to your Node.js apps.

Now, let's create our CSS. In the /public/css folder we created earlier, create a new file called **style.css**:

```css
body{font-size:12pt;font-family:helvetica}
.chatWindow{float:left;margin:20px;border:1px solid #000;width:
300px;background:#e5e5e5;border-radius:5px}
.chatName{margin-bottom:10px;background:#666;color:#fff;padding:4px}
.messages{padding:4px}
.message_outbound{color:blue;text-align:right}
.tstamp{font-size:9px;padding:2px;margin-bottom:10px;border-
bottom:1px dotted #666;color:#666}
.error{color:red;text-align:center}
.messageForm textarea{float:left;width:220px;margin:5px}
```

Lastly, we want to set up the brains of our app. We've saved the biggest file for last.

In the **public/js** folder, create a new file called **chat.js**:

```
chat.js
var chatManager = function(flybaseRef) {
    this.flybaseRef = flybaseRef;
};

chatManager.prototype = {
    chats: [],
    getChat: function(fromNumber) {
        var foundChat = null;
        for (c = 0; c < this.chats.length; c++) {
            if (this.chats[c].from == fromNumber) {
                foundChat = this.chats[c];
            }
        }
```

```
                    if (foundChat == null) {
                          foundChat = new chat( this.flybaseRef );
                          foundChat.init(fromNumber);
                          foundChat.displayTemplate();
                          this.chats.push(foundChat);
                    }
                return foundChat;
        },
        updateChats: function() {
              var _this = this;
              this.flybaseRef.once('value', function (data) {
                    data.forEach( function(message){
                          var row = message.value();
                          _this.getChat( row.fromNumber
                          ).addMessage(
                                row.textMessage,
                                row.tstamp,
                                row.direction
                          );
                    });
              });
              this.flybaseRef.on('added', function (data) {
                    var row = data.value();
                    _this.getChat( row.fromNumber ).addMessage(
                          row.textMessage,
                          row.tstamp,
                          row.direction
                    );
              });
        }
};
```

```javascript
var chat = function(flybaseRef) {
    this.flybaseRef = flybaseRef;
};
chat.prototype = {
    init: function(name) {
        this.from = name;
        this.chatName = 'chat-' + this.from;
        this.buttonName = 'submit-' + this.from;
        this.textName = 'reply-' + this.from;
    },
    replyMessage: function(message) {
        var _this = this;
        $.ajax({
            type: "POST",
            url: "/reply",
            data: {
                'To': this.from,
                'Body': message,
                'From': this.from
            },
            dataType: "json",
            success: function(data) {
                // your message was sent
            }
        });
    },
    displayTemplate: function() {
        var content = '<div class="chatName">Chat with ' +
        this.from + '</div> \
        <div class="messages" id="' + this.chatName + '">
        </div> \
```

```
        <div class="messageForm"><textarea id="' + this.
        textName + '"></textarea><button id="' + this.
        buttonName + '">Reply</button></div> \
    </div>';

        content = '<div class="chatWindow" id="' + this.
        tmplName + '">' + content + '</div>';

        $('#templateContainer').append(content);
        var _this = this;

        $('#' + this.buttonName).click(function() {
            _this.replyMessage($('#' + _this.textName).
            val());
            $('#' + _this.textName).val('');
        });
    },
    addMessage: function(message, tstamp, direction) {
        $('#' + this.chatName).append("<div
        class='message_" + direction + "'>" + message +
        "<div class='tstamp'>" + tstamp + "</div></div>");
    }
};
```

Our **chatManage** class is set up so that when it loads, it first grabs a list of saved text messages using the value event trigger and displays them by the phone number they were sent from.

We treat all messages to and from the same number as one session, so for each chat session, we would see a box displaying the messages between the agent and the customer and a textbox to use to send new messages.

We then listen for any new messages to come in using the added event trigger, and we then display them inside the proper chat box.

The chat class tells our app how to display the chat boxes and how to handle sending new replies.

In this case, when a message is sent by an agent, we post it to our backend /reply route, where it is saved to our Flybase app and then sent to the customer as a text message.

We're also storing the direction a message came from, either inbound or outbound. This way we can style each message to appear similar to when you view a chat log on your phone. The customer's texts will appear on the left side, and the agent's replies will appear on the right side.

Now let's fire up our app:

```javascript
node app.js
```

We've told our app to run on port 8080, so if you go to your web browser and type in http://localhost:8080/, you should see your call center.

Just an aside, if you're running this locally, you'll want to make sure you've got ngrok running before you go to the next step. If you haven't used ngrok (https://ngrok.com/) before, Kevin Whinnery over at Twilio has put together a great tutorial (www.twilio.com/blog/2013/10/test-your-webhooks-locally-with-ngrok.html) to help you get started.

Summary

We did it! Now that you've built a simple SMS call center app (https://github.com/flybaseio/sms-contact), it's your chance to create something with it.

Take this project and roll with it. Some ideas are you could actually completely remove the /reply AJAX call and instead create an outbound text queue that would store the message and then add an added listener to the outbound collection that would both send the reply to the customer and add it into the message collection so it would appear in the chat window.

This would eliminate the need for that /reply AJAX call and also add some queue support in cases of sending out multiple replies to several customers at once.

CHAPTER 2

Building a Live Blogging Tool

Live blogging is pretty handy when attending events; it never hurts to be able to live blog about the latest new gadgets as they are announced.

We're going to build a simple live blogging app using Node.js, Flybase, and Twilio.

This particular live blog solution is set up for one event. This means all posts to the phone number we specify will show up.

You could build on this to allow for multiple events, but that's a little more than we want to dive into today.

The Setup

We'll be using a few tools to build this app. You'll want to have Twilio, Flybase, and Node.js set up before you continue on. If you haven't already, sign up (`https://app.flybase.io/signup`) for a free Flybase account now and then create a new app. You'll use your app for your live blog app.

Getting Started

We first need to set up our Node.js app. Besides the Twilio and Flybase modules, we'll be using the Express framework (`http://expressjs.com/`) to set up our node web server to receive the POST request from Twilio,

© Roger Stringer 2021

R. Stringer, *Real-Time Twilio and Flybase*, https://doi.org/10.1007/978-1-4842-7074-5_2

so we'll need to install the express package. We'll also be using the body-parser module, so we are going to install that as well.

Let's create our package.json file:

```json
{
    "name": "live-blog",
    "version": "0.0.1",
    "description": "Live Blog App powered by Flybase, Twilio
                    and Node.js",
    "main": "app.js",
    "repository": "https://github.com/flybase/live-blog",
    "scripts": {
            "test": "echo \"Error: no test specified\" &&
                    exit 1"
    },
    "keywords": [
        "Twilio",
        "Flybase",
        "sms"
    ],
    "author": "Roger Stringer",
    "license": "MIT",
    "dependencies": {
        "Twilio": "~1.6.0",
        "ejs": "~0.8.5",
        "express": "~3.4.8",
        "flybase": "~1.7.8",
        "node-buzz": "~1.1.0",
        "moment": "~2.5.1",
        "less-middleware": "~0.2.1-beta",
```

```
        "body-parser" : "~1.4.2",
        "method-override" : "~2.0.2"
    },
    "engines": {
        "node": "0.10.26"
    }
}
```

Save this file, and from the terminal, run the following command:

npm install

This will create a node_modules folder containing all of the modules we want to use.

The first file we want to create is config.js; this will hold our configuration information:

```javascript
module.exports = {
    // Twilio API keys
    Twilio: {   // Where you will put your Twilio Credentials
        sid: "ACCOUNTSID",
        token: "AUTHTOKEN",
        from_number: "YOUR-NUMBER"
    },
    flybase: {  // Where you will put your flybase credentials
            api_key: "YOUR-API-KEY",
            app_name: "YOUR-flybase-APP"
    },
    un: 'admin',
    pw: 'password'
};
```

This file is for our configuration. We can access anything in here at anytime by referencing the file and calling the keys. For example, to get our Flybase API Key, we would call

javascript

```javascript
var config = require('./config');
console.log( config.flybase.api_key );
```

Replace ACCOUNTSID, AUTHTOKEN, and YOUR-NUMBER with your Twilio credentials and a phone number in your Twilio account that you'll be using.

Then, replace YOUR-API-KEY and YOUR-flybase-APP with your Flybase API Key to use.

At the beginning of our **app.js** file, we'll need to require express and initialize it into a variable called **app**. We're also going to use the bodyParser middleware (https://github.com/expressjs/body-parser) to make it easy to use the data we'll be getting in our POST request.

Create a new file called **app.js** and require the twilio, express, and flybase packages:

javascript

```javascript
var express = require('express');
var bodyParser = require('body-parser');
var methodOverride = require('method-override');
var path = require('path');
var config = require('./config');

var app = express();
app.set('views', path.join(process.cwd(), 'views'));
app.set('view engine', 'ejs');
app.use(bodyParser.json());
app.use(bodyParser.urlencoded({ extended: true }));
```

```
app.use(express.static(__dirname + '/public')); // set the
                                                  static files
                                                  location /
                                                  public/img
                                                  will be /img
                                                  for users

var port = process.env.PORT || 8080; // set our port

var Twilio = require('Twilio');
var client = Twilio(config.Twilio.sid, config.Twilio.token );

var flybase = require('flybase');
var postsRef = flybase.init(config.flybase.app_name, "posts",
config.flybase.api_key);
```

Flybase uses collections to organize data inside apps, so one app could have several collections. If you're familiar with relational databases, this is the equivalent of a table.

We'll be using one collection for our project, which we will call posts.

Let's set up our folder structure. Create a folder called views; this is where we will keep our frontend.

Create a file called index.ejs in the views folder:

HTML

```
<!doctype html>
<html>
<head>
        <link href='http://fonts.googleapis.com/css?family=L
        ato:400,300italic,400italic&subset=latin,latin-ext'
        rel='stylesheet' type='text/css'>
        <link rel="stylesheet" href="http://maxcdn.bootstrapcdn.
        com/bootstrap/3.2.0/css/bootstrap.min.css">
```

```html
        <script src="https://ajax.googleapis.com/ajax/libs/
        jquery/1.7.2/jquery.min.js"></script>
        <script src="https://cdn.flybase.io/flybase.
        js?latest=1"></script>
        <title>Live Blog, powered by Flybase and Twilio</title>
</head>
<body>
        <div class='container'>
            <div class="row">
                <div class="col-md-4">
                    <div id="postsDiv"></div>
                </div>
        </div>
        <script>
            $(function(){
                var postsRef = new flybase("<%= apikey %>",
                "<%= appname %>", "posts");
                postsRef.once('value', function (data) {
                    console.log( "we found " + data.count()
                    + " posts");
                    data.forEach( function(post){
                        displayPost(post.value() );
                    });
                });

                postsRef.on('added', function (data) {
                    var post = data.value();
                    displayPost(post);
                });

                function displayPost(post) {
                    $('<div/>')
                        .attr("id",post._id)
```

```
            .text(post.textMessage)
            .appendTo( $('#postsDiv') );
        $('#postsDiv')[0].scrollTop =
        $('#postsDiv')[0].scrollHeight;
    }
  });
</script>
</body>
</html>
```

This will listen for any new post to our posts collection in our app and then output it on the screen as it happens. Now, let's set up our Twilio listener.

Setting Up Our Twilio Listener

Twilio uses webhooks (https://en.wikipedia.org/wiki/Webhook) to let your server know when an incoming message or phone call comes into our app. We need to set up an endpoint that we can tell Twilio to use for the messaging webhook.

We're going to add a route for /**message** that responds with some TwiML (www.twilio.com/docs/api/twiml). TwiML is a basic set of instructions you can use to tell Twilio what to do when you receive an incoming call or SMS message. Our code will look like this:

```javascript
// backend routes

// listen for incoming sms messages
app.post('/message', function (request, response) {
    var d = new Date();
    var date = d.toLocaleString();
```

```
var postBody = request.param('Body');

var numMedia = parseInt( request.param('NumMedia') );
var i;
if (numMedia > 0) {
    for (i = 0; i < numMedia; i++) {
        var mediaUrl = request.param('MediaUrl' + i);
        postBody += '<br /><img src="' +
        mediaUrl + '" />';
    }
}

postsRef.push({
    sid: request.param('MessageSid'),
    type:'text',
    tstamp: date,
    fromNumber:request.param('From'),
    textMessage:postBody,
    fromCity:request.param('FromCity'),
    fromState:request.param('FromState'),
    fromCountry:request.param('FromCountry')
});

var resp = new Twilio.TwimlResponse();
resp.message('Post received');
response.writeHead(200, {  // 200 is the limit for the
                                    title of the blog
    'Content-Type':'text/xml'
});
response.end(resp.toString());
});
```

This will store our message in our posts collection. It will check to see if there are any images attached to the message, and if there are, it will append them to the message body.

Finally, let's set our server to listen on port 8080 and tell it what to do when we view it from a browser:

```javascript
// frontend routes

app.get('*', function(req, res) {
    res.render('index', {
            apikey:config.flybase.api_key,
            appname:config.flybase.app_name,
    });
});

var server = app.listen(port, function() {
    console.log('Listening on port %d', server.address().
    port);
});
```

You can then call node app.js from your terminal, and it will load the app.

Send an SMS message to your Twilio number, and you should get a response back. If you don't, take a look at the Twilio App Monitor (www.twilio.com/user/account/developer-tools/app-monitor) to help determine what went wrong.

Summary

We've now built a basic live blogging tool. Nothing too fancy, but you can take it from here and build on it to make something more fancy. Live blogging is handy for attending events. You could set it up to let attendees make live posts as they attend sessions or live blog about the latest news at a press event. We'll build on this later to include an "Ionic" app to handle the posts.

CHAPTER 3

Building a Real-Time Group Chat App

Last November, I went to a conference with several coworkers, and we wanted to keep everyone up to date and organized to keep track of what our plans were.

We set up a group chat system that let one of the members send an SMS and everyone else get the message, and if someone replied, we'd all see the reply.

That was handy, and today, I'm going to show you how to build a similar web app. The app will consist of a simple control panel where you can manage who is part of a group and a backend that will handle incoming and outgoing text messages and route them to the proper group members.

You will also be able to send and receive messages from a page on the site in real time, for when you may not have your phone on you but want to send a message to the group and vice versa.

Ingredients

You'll want to have these set up before you continue on.

We'll use Flybase (`http://flybase.io/`) to handle the data storage and real-time aspects of the app, Twilio (`www.twilio.com/`) to handle the actual SMS work, and Node.js for the system itself.

© Roger Stringer 2021

R. Stringer, *Real-Time Twilio and Flybase*, https://doi.org/10.1007/978-1-4842-7074-5_3

We're going to build this particular app for one single group, but it wouldn't be hard to extend it for multiple groups.

Then finally, we'll host this app on Heroku as a free app (`https://heroku.com/`, a handy hosting platform for getting your projects up and running quickly, especially handy when combined with Flybase and Twilio).

Node.js will be the backend portion of our app; it's where we will build our listeners for Twilio to talk to whenever we send or receive a text message.

Flybase is a real-time app platform and will be our datastore of choice for our app. It will be used to manage who is a member of a group and to store incoming and outgoing messages and whom they came from. If you haven't already, sign up (`https://app.flybase.io/signup`) for a free Flybase account now and then create a new app from inside your dashboard. You'll use this app for your group chat system.

Twilio is our ever-handy phone API, which lets us build services like a group chat app or even a call center. Don't have a Twilio account yet? Sign up for free (`www.twilio.com/try-twilio`).

Getting Started

We first need to set up our Node.js app.

Besides the Twilio and Flybase modules, we'll be using the Express framework (`http://expressjs.com/`) to set up our node web server to receive the POST request from Twilio, so we'll need to install the express package. We'll also be using the body-parser module, so we are going to install that as well.

Let's create our package.json file:

```javascript
{
  "name": "group-chat",
  "version": "0.0.1",
  "description": "SMS Group Chat powered by Flybase, Twilio and
                  Node.js",
  "main": "app.js",
  "repository": "https://github.com/flybaseio/group-chat",
  "scripts": {
    "test": "echo \"Error: no test specified\" && exit 1"
  },
  "keywords": [
    "twilio",
    "flybase",
    "sms"
  ],
  "author": "Roger Stringer",
  "license": "MIT",
  "dependencies": {
    "body-parser": "~1.16.0",
    "ejs": "~2.5.5",
    "express": "~4.14.0",
    "flybase": "^1.8.2",
    "less-middleware": "~2.2.0",
    "method-override": "~2.3.7",
    "moment": "~2.17.1",
    "node-buzz": "~1.1.0",
    "twilio": "~2.11.1"
  }
}
```

Save this file, and from the terminal, run the following command:

```javascript
npm install
```

This will create a node_modules folder containing all of the modules we want to use.

Let's set up our folder structure and create a folder called views. This is where we will keep our frontend.

Now, create a folder called public. This will host our static files. Inside that folder, create a css folder and a js folder. We'll come back to these later.

The first file we want to create is config.js; this will hold our configuration information:

```javascript
module.exports = {
    // Twilio API keys
    twilio: {
        sid: "ACCOUNTSID",
        token: "AUTHTOKEN",
        from_number: "YOUR-NUMBER"
    },
    flybase: {
            api_key: "YOUR-API-KEY",
            app_name: "YOUR-FLYBASE-APP"
    },
    un: 'admin',
    pw: 'password'
};
```

This file is for our configuration. We can access anything in here at anytime by referencing the file and calling the keys. For example, to get our Flybase API Key, we would call

```javascript
var config = require('./config');
console.log( config.flybase.api_key );
```

Replace ACCOUNTSID, AUTHTOKEN, and YOUR-NUMBER with your Twilio credentials and a phone number in your Twilio account that you'll be using.

Then, replace YOUR-API-KEY and YOUR-FLYBASE-APP with your Flybase API Key.

At the beginning of our app.js file, we'll need to require express and initialize it into a variable called app. We're also going to use the bodyParser middleware (https://github.com/expressjs/body-parser) to make it easy to use the data we'll be getting in our POST request.

Create a new file called app.js and require the twilio, express, and flybase packages:

```javascript
var express = require('express');
var bodyParser = require('body-parser');
var methodOverride = require('method-override');
var path = require('path');
var config = require('./config');

var app = express();
app.set('views', path.join(process.cwd(), 'views'));
app.set('view engine', 'ejs');
app.use(bodyParser.json());
app.use(bodyParser.urlencoded( extended: true }));
app.use(express.static(__dirname + '/public')); // set the
static files location /public/img will be /img for users

var port = process.env.PORT || 8080; // set our port
```

```
var twilio = require('twilio');
var client = twilio(config.twilio.sid, config.twilio.token );

var flybase = require('flybase');
var messagesRef = flybase.init(config.flybase.app_name,
                  "messages", config.flybase.api_key);
var groupRef = flybase.init(config.flybase.app_name, "groups",
                  config.flybase.api_key);
```

Flybase uses collections to organize data inside apps, so one app could have several collections. If you're familiar with relational databases, this is the equivalent of a table.

We'll be using two collections for our project: one will contain messages, and the other will contain groups. With that in mind, we've created two different references to our Flybase app, one for messages and one for our group. This is the start of our app. Next, we'll build our web interface to manage group members and also allow for sending and receiving messages.

After that, we'll build our Twilio interface, and you'll have a fun app to play with.

Sending and Receiving Texts

We'll need to add a few things to send and receive texts. Our first step is to add a listener for Twilio.

Twilio uses webhooks (https://en.wikipedia.org/wiki/Webhook) to let your server know when an incoming message or phone call comes into our app. We need to set up an endpoint that we can tell Twilio to use for the messaging webhook.

We're going to add a route for /message that responds with some TwiML (www.twilio.com/docs/api/twiml). TwiML is a basic set of

instructions you can use to tell Twilio what to do when you receive an
incoming call or SMS message. Our code will look like this:

```javascript
// listen for incoming sms messages
app.post('/message', function (request, response) {

    groupRef.where( {"memberNumber":request.param('From')}
).limit(1).on( "value", function ( data ){
        if( data.count() ){
            data.forEach( function( snapshot ){
                var member = snapshot.value();
                messagesRef.push({
                    sid: request.param('MessageSid'),
                    type:'text',
                  tstamp: new Date().toLocaleString(),
                    fromName:member.memberName,
                    fromNumber:request.param('From'),
                    message:request.param('Body'),
                    media:"",
                    fromCity:request.
                    param('FromCity'),
                    fromState:request.
                    param('FromState'),
                    fromCountry:request.
                    param('FromCountry'),
                    groupNumber:request.param('To')
                });
            });
        }
});
```

```
var numMedia = parseInt( request.param('NumMedia') );
if (numMedia > 0) {
    for (i = 0; i < numMedia; i++) {
        var mediaUrl = request.param('MediaUrl' + i);
        groupRef.where( {"memberNumber":request.
        param('From')} ).limit(1).on( "value",
        function ( data ){
            if( data.count() ){
                data.forEach( function( snapshot ){
                    var member = snapshot.value();
                    messagesRef.push({
                        sid: request.
                        param('MessageSid'),
                        type:'text',
                        tstamp: new Date().
                        toLocaleString(),
                        fromName:member.
                        memberName,
                        fromNumber:request.
                        param('From'),
                        message:"",
                        media:mediaUrl,
                        fromCity:request.
                        param('FromCity'),
                        fromState:request.
                        param('FromState'),
                        fromCountry:request.
                        param('FromCountry'),
                        groupNumber:request.
                        param('To')
```

```
                                    });
                        });
                }
            });
        }
    }
    var resp = new twilio.TwimlResponse();
    resp.message('Message received.');
    response.writeHead(200, {
        'Content-Type':'text/xml'
    });
    response.end(resp.toString());
});
```

This will listen for any incoming SMS messages and store them inside your Flybase app, specifically inside the messages collection.

As part of storing the message, we perform a lookup to find the groups member with the same phone number the message was sent from. We then use this lookup to verify the member is part of the group and also to get the member's name.

If no member was found, then no message gets sent.

Once a message has been received, we use the Twilio node library to initialize a new **TwimlResponse**. We then use the message keyword (www.twilio.com/docs/api/twiml/sms/message) to set what we want to respond to the message with. In this case, we'll just say "Message received."

We'll then set the content-type of our response to text/xml and send the string representation of the TwimlResponse we built.

Listening for Changes

As part of our `app.js` code, we also want to add some asynchronous listeners to listen for changes to our Flybase app:

```javascript
// when a new message is added to the Flybase app, send it via
    Twilio...
messagesRef.on("added", function (data ){
    var snapshot = data.value();
    sendMessage(
        snapshot.groupNumber,
        snapshot.fromName,
        snapshot.fromNumber,
        snapshot.message,
        snapshot.media || ""
    );
});

groupRef.on("added", function ( data ){
    var snapshot = data.value();
    var msg = snapshot.memberName + ' has joined the group';
    messagesRef.push({
        sid: "",
        type:'',
        tstamp: new Date().toLocaleString(),
        fromName:"Admin",
        fromNumber:"",
        message:msg,
        media:"",
        fromCity:"",
        fromState:"",
```

```
            fromCountry:"",
            groupNumber:snapshot.groupNumber
      });
});

groupRef.on("removed", function ( data ){
      var snapshot = data.value();
      var msg = snapshot.memberName + ' has left the group';
      //      send broadcast that a group member has been removed
      messagesRef.push({
            sid: "",
            type:'',
            tstamp: new Date().toLocaleString(),
            fromName:"Admin",
            fromNumber:"",
            message:msg,
            media:"",
            fromCity:"",
            fromState:"",
            fromCountry:"",
            groupNumber:snapshot.groupNumber
      });

});


//      broadcast a message to the group
function sendMessage( group_number, from_name, from_number,
message, media ){
      var msg = from_name + ": " + message;
      groupRef.where( {"memberNumber":{"$not":from_number}} ).on
      ( "value", function ( data ){
```

```
    if( data.count() ){
        data.forEach( function( snapshot ){
            var member = snapshot.value();
            var msgObj = {
                to:member.memberNumber,
                from:group_number,
                body:msg
            };
            if( media !== "" ){
                msgObj.mediaUrl = media;
            }
            client.sendMessage( msgObj, function(
            err, data ) {});
        });
    }
});
}
```

We've set up three asynchronous listeners, one for the **messages** collection, which listens for any messages being "added" to it and, when it receives a notification of a new message, calls our **sendMessage** function to send the message to the other members of the group.

The other two asynchronous listeners are for our **groups** collection: the first one listens for any new members being added to a group and then sends an announcement that the member has joined the group.

The last listener will listen for any members being "removed" from a group and sends an announcement that the member has left the group.

Finally, our **sendMessage** function is used for sending messages on to the other group members; it will perform a query to return all members of the group, excluding the person who sent the message, and send the message on to each member.

Messages will appear formatted with the member's name followed by the message:

```
John: How about pizza after work?
```

Finally, let's set our server to listen on port 8080 and tell it what to do when we view it from a browser:

```javascript
// frontend routes ============================

// Create basic  middleware used to authenticate all admin
   requests
var auth = express.basicAuth(config.un, config.pw);

// route to handle all frontend requests with a password to
   protect unauthorized access....
app.get('*', auth, function(req, res) {
    res.render('index', {
        api_key:config.flybase.api_key,
        app_name:config.flybase.app_name,
        group_number:config.twilio.from_number
    });
});

var server = app.listen(port, function() {
    console.log('Listening on port %d', server.address().
    port);
});
```

This is the backend portion of our group chat app. It listens for incoming text messages, stores them in our Flybase app, and then sends them to the other members of the group.

Now, we need to build our control panel, where the admin can manage group members and also send and receive messages.

Managing Your Group

We're going to build a simple web interface to manage our group members.

The data we store for our group members will consist of the following three pieces of data:

- Group phone number (the Twilio number we stored in the **twilio_number** variable in the "Getting Started" section)

- Member name

- Member phone number

We'll also display a basic chat box that will let our admin send messages and see what messages are being sent.

First, let's create our view. In the /views folder, create a file called index.ejs:

`

```
HTML
<!doctype html>
<html>
<head>
    <link href='//fonts.googleapis.com/css?family=Lat
    o:400,300italic,400italic&subset=latin,latin-ext'
    rel='stylesheet' type='text/css'>
    <link rel="stylesheet" type="text/css" href="//angular-
    ui.github.com/ng-grid/css/ng-grid.css" />
    <link rel="stylesheet" href="//maxcdn.bootstrapcdn.com/
    bootstrap/3.2.0/css/bootstrap.min.css">
    <link href="//maxcdn.bootstrapcdn.com/font-awesome/4.3.0/
    css/font-awesome.min.css" rel="stylesheet">
```

```html
<link rel="stylesheet" type="text/css" href="/css/style.
css">

<script src="https://ajax.googleapis.com/ajax/libs/
jquery/1.7.2/jquery.min.js"></script>
<script src="https://cdn.flybase.io/flybase.
js?20150217"></script>
<script src="https://cdn.flybase.io/libs/phone.js"></
script>
<script src="/js/group.js"></script>

<title>Group Chat, powered by Flybase and Twilio</title>
</head>
<body>
<div class='container'>
    <div class="row">
        <div class="col-md-6">
            <h3>Group Members</h3>
            <div id="group_wrapper"></div>
            <hr />
            <h2>Add new member</h2>
            <div class="well">
                <form id="group_form"
                method="post" accept-
                charset="utf-8" class="form-
                inline">
                    <div class="form-group">
                        <div class="input-
                        group">
```

```
                        <div class=
                        "input-group-
                        addon"><i class=
                        "fa fa-pencil">
                        </i></div>
                        <input type=
                        "text" class=
                        "form-control"
                        id="name"
                        name="name"
                        placeholder=
                        "name">
                </div>
        </div>
        <div class="form-group">
                <div class="input-
                group">
                        <div class=
                        "input-group-
                        addon"><i class=
                        "fa fa-mobile">
                        </i></div>
                        <input type=
                        "tel" class=
                        "form-control"
                        id="phone"
                        name="phone"
                        placeholder=
                        "+11112223333"/>
                </div>
        </div>
```

```
                <button type="submit"
                class="btn btn-primary">
                Save</button>
            </form>
        </div>
    </div>
    <div class="col-md-4 col-md-offset-1">
        <div id="chatBox" class='chat'>
            <header>Chat Log</header>
            <ul id='messagesDiv' class='chat-
            messages'></ul>
            <footer>
                <form id="msg_form"
                method="post" accept-
                charset="utf-8"
                class="form-inline">
                    <input type="text"
                    id="messageInput"
                    placeholder="Type a
                    message..." />
                </form>
            </footer>
        </div>
    </div>
</div>
<script>
    $(function(){
//          initialize our Flybase object
            var myGroupManager = new groupManager( "<%=
            api_key %>", "<%= app_name %>", "<?%= group_
            number %>");
```

```
                    myGroupManager.start();
         });
      </script>
  </body>
</html>
```

This will display our control panel, which will be split into two panes, the left side for viewing group members and the right side for viewing the chat log.

At the bottom of the page, we're initializing our groupManager class. We'll create that file shortly.

Next, let's create our style sheet. In the public/css folder, create a file called style.css:

```css
body{font-size:12pt;font-family:helvetica}
.chatWindow{float:left;margin:20px;border:1px solid #000;
width:300px;background:#e5e5e5;border-radius:5px}
.chatName{margin-bottom:10px;background:#666;color:#fff;
padding:4px}
.messages{padding:4px}
.message_outbound{color:blue;text-align:right}
.tstamp{font-size:9px;padding:2px;margin-bottom:10px;
border-bottom:1px dotted #666;color:#666}
.error{color:red;text-align:center}
.messageForm textarea{float:left;width:220px;margin:5px}
#phone{width:140px;}
#chatBox{background-color: #f8f8f8;background: rgb(229, 228,
228);margin:10px;}
.hide {display: none; }
.chat {font-family: "Helvetica Neue Light", "Helvetica Neue",
Helvetica, Arial, "Lucida Grande", sans-serif;
border-radius: 3px;-webkit-box-shadow: 0px 8px 20px rgba(0, 0,
```

```
0, 0.2);box-shadow: 0px 8px 20px rgba(0, 0, 0, 0.2);
background-color: #dfe3ea;border: 1px solid #CCC;overflow:
auto;padding: 0px;font-size: 18px;line-height: 22px;color:
#666; }
.chat header {background-color: #EEE;background: -webkit-
gradient(linear, left top, left bottom, from(#EEEEEE),
to(#DDDDDD));background: -webkit-linear-gradient(top, #EEEEEE,
#DDDDDD);background: linear-gradient(top, #EEEEEE, #DDDDDD);-
webkit-box-shadow: inset 0px 1px 0px rgba(255, 255, 255,
0.9), 0px 1px 2px rgba(0, 0, 0, 0.1);box-shadow: inset 0px
1px 0px rgba(255, 255, 255, 0.9), 0px 1px 2px rgba(0, 0,
0, 0.1);border-radius: 3px 3px 0px 0px;border-bottom: 1px
solid #CCC;line-height: 24px;font-size: 12px;text-align:
center;color: #999; }
.chat input {-webkit-box-sizing: border-box;-moz-box-sizing:
border-box;box-sizing: border-box;-webkit-box-shadow: inset
0px 1px 3px rgba(0, 0, 0, 0.2);box-shadow: inset 0px 1px 3px
rgba(0, 0, 0, 0.2);border-radius: 3px;padding: 0px 10px;
height: 30px;font-size: 18px;width: 100%;font-weight:
normal;outline: none; }
.chat .chat-toolbar {background-color: #FFF;padding:
10px;position: relative;border-bottom: 1px solid #CCC; }
.chat .chat-toolbar label {text-transform: uppercase;line-
height: 32px;font-size: 14px;color: #999;position:
absolute;top: 10px;left: 20px;z-index: 1; }
.chat .chat-toolbar input {-webkit-box-shadow: none;box-shadow:
none;border: 1px solid #FFF;padding-left: 100px;color: #999; }
.chat .chat-toolbar input:active, .chat .chat-toolbar
input:focus {color: #1d9dff;border: 1px solid #FFF; }
.chat ul {list-style: none;margin: 0px;padding: 20px;height:
200px;overflow: auto; }
```

```
.chat ul li {margin-bottom: 10px;line-height: 24px; }
.chat ul li:last-child {margin: 0px; }
.chat ul .chat-username {margin-right: 10px; }
.chat footer {display: block;padding: 10px; }
.chat footer input {border: 1px solid #ced3db;height: 40px;
width:75%;}
```

Now, let's move on to the brains of our system. Inside the public/js folder, we'll create a file called group.js:

```javascript
var groupManager = function(api_key, app_name, group_number) {
//      store the group number
        this.group_number = group_number;
//      reference to our messages collection...
        this.messagesRef = new Flybase(api_key, app_name,
        "messages");

//      reference to our group collection...
        this.groupRef = new Flybase(api_key, app_name, "groups");

        this.group_members = [];
};
```

This is the first part of our **groupManager** class. So far, we've told it to start up two Flybase references, one called messagesRef and one called groupRef. We also stored our group number as a variable called group_number.

Now, let's set up our actions:

```javascript
groupManager.prototype.start = function(){
     var _this = this;

// list group members if any
     this.groupRef.on("value", function( data ){
```

```
    if( data.count() ){
        data.forEach( function( snapshot ){
            var member = snapshot.value();
            _this.group_members[member._id] = member;
        });
    }
    _this.displayGroup();
});

// listen for new members being added
    this.groupRef.on("added", function( snapshot ){
        var member = snapshot.value();
        _this.group_members[member._id] = member;
        _this.displayGroup();
    });

// save new group member to our app
    $("#group_form").submit( function(e){
        e.preventDefault();
        var member = {
            'groupNumber': _this.group_number,
            'memberName': $("#name").val(),
            'memberNumber': clean_phone( $("#phone").val() )
        };
        _this.groupRef.push( member );
        $("#name").val('');
        $("#phone").val('');
        return false;
    });

// listen for members being removed
    $('div').on('click','a.delete', function(e){
        var _id = e.target.id;
```

```
            _this.groupRef.remove(_id);
            return false;
    });

    this.groupRef.on("removed", function( snapshot ){
            var member = snapshot.value();
            _this.group_members[member._id] = undefined;
            _this.displayGroup();
    });

// list any existing chat message
    this.messagesRef.on('value', function (data) {
            if( data.count() ){
                    data.forEach( function(message){
                            _this.displayChatMessage(message.value() );
                    });
            }
    });

// listen for incoming chat messages
    this.messagesRef.on('added', function (data) {
            var message = data.value();
            _this.displayChatMessage( message );
    });

// listen for outgoing chat messages
    $('#msg_form').submit( function(e){
            e.preventDefault();
            var message = {
                            "tstamp": new Date().toLocaleString(),
                            "fromName": "Admin",
                            "fromNumber": "",
                            "message": $('#messageInput').val(),
                            "fromCity": "",
```

```
                    "fromState": "",
                    "fromCountry": "",
                    "groupNumber": _this.group_number
            }
            _this.messagesRef.push( message );
            $('#messageInput').val('');
            return false;
        });
};
```

Our function sets up our asynchronous listeners, as well as listeners for form submissions and members being deleted by pressing the delete button.

If a group member is added, then the member will be added to the **groups** collection, and a notification will be sent to the other members of the group. The listing of group members will also show the new member.

If a person is removed, their name will vanish from the list, and a message will be sent to the remaining group members.

The other side of our **groupManager** class is the actual chatting side of our program. When the admin types in a message, it will get sent to the other group members. At the same time, when another group member sends a message, the admin will see the message in the chat box.

We have two functions left: one to display all members of a group and the other to display chat messages.

For our groups, we store information in a class-wide variable called **group_members**. This lets us quickly add, update, or remove members as we receive notifications about it:

```javascript
// Display group members
groupManager.prototype.displayGroup = function(){
    $('#group_wrapper').html('');
```

```
for (var i in this.group_members ) {
    var member = this.group_members[i];
    if( member !== undefined ){
        var html = '';
        html = '<span>'+member.memberName+'
        ( ' + member.memberNumber + ' )</span>
        <a href="#delete" class="delete" id="' +
        member._id+'">[remove]</a>';
        $('<div/>').prepend( html ).appendTo
        ($('#group_wrapper'));
    }
}
};
```

Our last function displays each chat message as it is received:

```javascript
// Display chat messages
groupManager.prototype.displayChatMessage = function( message )
{
    var _this = this;
    var msg = message.message;
    if( message.media !== "" ){
        msg += '<br /><img src="' + message.media + '" />';
    }
    $('<li/>')
        .attr("id",message._id)
        .html(msg)
        .prepend(
            $("<strong class='example-chat-username' />").
            text(message.fromName+': ')
            ).appendTo( $('#messagesDiv') );
```

```
$('#messagesDiv')[0].scrollTop = $('#messagesDiv')[0].
scrollHeight;
};
```

One last thing to do is to start our app:

```
javascript
node app.js
```

We've told our app to run on port 8080, so if you go to your web browser and type in `http://localhost:8080/`, you should see your group chat.

Hosting It on Heroku

Heroku is great for making server configurations easy and painless. We can build faster and worry about the things that matter to us instead of trying to configure our own servers. This works perfectly with our philosophy here at Flybase and lets us build things quickly. Let's look at how we can deploy our group chat app to Heroku in mere seconds.

Go ahead and go to `http://heroku.com` and create your free account. The dashboard is incredibly simple and user-friendly.

Next, you'll want to install the Heroku Toolbelt. The Heroku Toolbelt will give us access to the Heroku Command Line Utility. The Heroku Toolbelt program comes in different operating systems, which you can download from the links provided in the following:

- Mac (`https://devcenter.heroku.com/toolbelt-downloads/osx`)

- Windows (`https://devcenter.heroku.com/toolbelt-downloads/windows`)

- Debian/Ubuntu (`https://devcenter.heroku.com/toolbelt-downloads/debian`)

After we install the Toolbelt, we'll have access to the **heroku** command. Now, you'll want to perform the following operations:

1. `git init` inside the folder you created your group chat app in to create a new git repository

2. `heroku login` to log into Heroku

3. `heroku create` to create the application within Heroku

4. `git push heroku master` to push your group chat repository to Heroku

5. `heroku ps:scale web=1` to tell Heroku to create a dyno (a worker, to respond to web requests)

6. `heroku open` to open your web browser at your new custom URL

And that's it. Your app is now running on Heroku.

Assigning Your Group Chat to a Phone Number in Twilio

Now, we want to go back to our Twilio account and open the phone number we were using to send messages.

When you create your app on Heroku, you can give it a unique URL. For example, let's say

`https://my-group-chat.herokuapp.com/`

Our URL to receive messages via SMS will now be `https://my-group-chat.herokuapp.com/message`.

Now send an SMS message to your Twilio number, and you should get a response back. If you don't, take a look at the Twilio App Monitor (`www.twilio.com/user/account/developer-tools/app-monitor`) to help determine what went wrong.

Summary

We've built a real-time group chat app using Flybase (`http://flybase.io`) and Twilio (`http://twilio.com`).

This group chat app can even handle incoming media (pictures, Word docs, videos, etc.) from Twilio and resend it on to the rest of the group.

You can find our group chat app here at GitHub (`https://github.com/flybaseio/group-chat`).

This app can be used for a group of people to carry on a conversation. This can be handy when attending events.

You could use this to notify attendees of upcoming talks. For example, a conference could add their attendees to a group and then send a broadcast when it is time for a talk to begin, when it is lunchtime, or for an emergency.

CHAPTER 4

Creating a Click-to-Call Call Center

This chapter covers some interesting areas of both Flybase and Twilio. We're going to build a "click-to-call" call center, where visitors can click a product on a page and begin a Twilio Client call with agents on another web page. To do this, we are going to use Flybase's custom events.

This tutorial is based on a post (www.twilio.com/blog/2014/07/creating-a-click-to-call-service-with-twilio-client-pusher-and-python.html) from Twilio last year on using Pusher, Twilio, and Python to build a similar system, but ours will be a little simpler, thanks to having fewer systems involved.

Flybase's Custom Events

Flybase gives developers a lot of neat tools to use. In this tutorial, we are going to build a custom "click-to-call" call center using Flybase's custom events.

What are custom events? You know about the reserved events (http://flybase.io/docs/web/guide/reading-data.html) such as value, added, changed, online, or removed, but we also have custom events. Custom events can be handy for passing messages or data between devices, users, different collections, or even different parts of the same app.

Here's one basic example of a custom event listener:

```javascript
flybase.on("custom_event", function(message) {
    console.log( message );
});

flybase.trigger("custom_event", "Hi")
```

Custom events are meant to be used when you want to pass data between devices but don't necessarily need to save the data anywhere. In this case, it works more as a signaling server, letting devices know something is happening.

What Is a Click-to-Call System?

"Click to call" allows customers to click a link and start an in-browser voice call with a human. While that voice call is being established, contextual information about the customer (such as the item they are looking at or their name/interests/Facebook likes) is passed over to the person handling the call, who can then provide a highly personalized experience. The customer doesn't need to tell them their name or the product/service they're interested in: click to call does this all for you. It gets rid of the annoying parts of call centers and lets you get on with what's important to you.

Necessary Tools

We'll be using the following tools in this chapter:

- Twilio lets us build services like an SMS app or even a call center.

- Flybase will be used to manage who is a member of a group and to store incoming and outgoing messages and whom they came from.

- Node.js will be the backend portion of our app; it's where we will build our listeners for Twilio to talk to whenever we send or receive a text message.

Setting Up Twilio Client

Let's start by creating a **TwiML** app, an app which can be reused for TwiML configuration that can be applied to Twilio phone numbers or TwiML applications. Each TwiML app has a unique SID that we use to generate security tokens for Twilio Client.

Head over to the apps page (`www.twilio.com/user/account/apps`) on your account and create a new app by clicking "Create TwiML App."

We're calling our **TwiML** app "Click-to-Call Demo." You'll need to link the Voice Request URL to a URL on your website. We'll click Save, and this will generate an SID for the TwiML app that we will use later on, so keep it handy.

Getting Started

We first need to set up our *Node.js* app.

Besides the Twilio and Flybase modules, we'll be using the Express framework (`http://expressjs.com/`) to set up our node web server to receive the POST request from Twilio, so we'll need to install the express package. We'll also be using the **body-parser** module, so we are going to install that as well.

Let's create our **package.json** file:

```javascript
{
    "name": "call-ads",
    "version": "0.0.1",
```

```
"description": "Click-to-call call Center powered by
                  Flybase, Twilio and Node.js",
"main": "app.js",
"repository": "https://github.com/flybaseio/call-ads",
"scripts": {
      "test": "echo \"Error: no test specified\" && exit 1"
},
"keywords": [
      "twilio",
      "data mcfly",
      "flybase",
      "twilio",
      "sms"
],
"author": "Roger Stringer",
"license": "MIT",
"dependencies": {
      "twilio": "~1.6.0",
    "ejs": "~0.8.5",
      "express": "~3.4.8",
      "flybase": "~1.5.2",
      "node-buzz": "~1.1.0",
      "moment": "~2.5.1",
      "less-middleware": "~0.2.1-beta",
      "body-parser" : "~1.4.2",
      "method-override" : "~2.0.2"
},
"engines": {
      "node": "0.12"
}
}
```

Save this file, and from the terminal, run the following command:

npm install

This will create a "node_modules" folder containing all of the modules
we want to use.

Let's set up our folder structure and create a folder called "views." This
is where we will keep our frontend. Now, create a folder called "public."
This will host our static files. Inside that folder, create an "images" folder;
we'll come back to it later in the chapter. The first file we want to create is
config.js. This will hold our configuration information:

```javascript
module.exports = {
    // Twilio API keys
    twilio: {
        sid: "ACCOUNT-SID",
        token: "AUTH-TOKEN",
        appid: 'YOUR-TWILIO-APP-ID'
    },
    //      Flybase settings
    flybase: {
        api_key: "YOUR-API-KEY",
        app_name: "YOUR-FLYBASE-APP"
    },
    //      Username and password for admin section.
    un: 'admin',
    pw: 'password'
};
```

This file is for our configuration. We can access anything in here at anytime by referencing the file and calling the keys. For example, to get our Flybase API Key, we would call

```
var config = require('./config');
console.log( config.flybase.api_key );
```

Replace **ACCOUNTSID**, **AUTHTOKEN**, **YOUR-TWILIO-APP-ID**, and **YOUR-NUMBER** with your Twilio credentials and a phone number in your Twilio account that you'll be using.

The **appid** variable, which is showing the placeholder of **YOUR-TWILIO-APP-ID**, is where you store the SID you created in the last step. Next, replace **YOUR-API-KEY** and **YOUR-FLYBASE-APP** with your Flybase API Key to use.

Finally, the **un** and **pw** variables are where you store a username and password to be used when accessing your control panel via the "/cc" route.

At the beginning of our **app.js** file, we'll need to require express and initialize it into a variable called app. We're also going to use the **bodyParser** middleware (https://github.com/expressjs/body-parser) to make it easy to use the data we'll be getting in our POST request.

Create a new file called **app.js** and require the twilio, express, and flybase packages:

```
var express = require('express');
var bodyParser = require('body-parser');
var methodOverride = require('method-override');
var path = require('path');
var config = require('./config');

var app = express();
app.set('views', path.join(process.cwd(), 'views'));
app.set('view engine', 'ejs');
app.use(bodyParser.json());
app.use(bodyParser.urlencoded({       extended: true       }));
```

```
app.use(express.static(__dirname + '/public')); // set the
static files location /public/img will be /img for users

var port = process.env.PORT || 5000; // set our port

var twilio = require('twilio');
var client = twilio(config.twilio.sid, config.twilio.token);

var flybase = require('flybase');
var leadsRef = flybase.init(config.flybase.app_name, "leads",
                config.flybase.api_key);
```

Flybase uses collections to organize data inside apps, so one app could have several collections. If you're familiar with relational databases, this is the equivalent of a table. We'll be using one collection for our project, called **leads**.

Custom events are likewise linked to the collection we connected to, so if we established a Flybase connection to leads, then we will listen for all events, reserved or otherwise, in the **leads** collection.

This is the start of our app. Next, we'll build our web interface to manage group members and also allow for sending and receiving messages. After that, we'll build our Twilio interface, and you'll have a fun app to play with:

javascript

```
//      listen for incoming sms messages
app.post('/voice', function (req, res) {
    leadsRef.trigger("new-caller", {
        item: req.param('item'),
        name:req.param('name')
    });

    res.writeHead(200, {
        'Content-Type':'text/xml'
    });
```

```
var resp = new twilio.TwimlResponse();
resp.dial(function() {
        this.client('Admin');
});

res.type('text/xml');
res.end( resp.toString() );
});
```

When we receive a new POST request to the /voice route, we store this in the **new-caller** event in our Flybase app and then connect the call to our admin user, whom we are calling "Admin" in this case.

Finally, we set up our frontend routes, /cc and /, and then tell our server to listen on port 5000 and tell it what to do when we view it from a browser:

```javascript
var auth = express.basicAuth(config.un, config.pw);

// route to handle all frontend requests, with a password to
   protect unauthorized access....
app.get('/cc', auth, function(req, res) {
    var capability = new twilio.Capability( config.twilio.
    sid, config.twilio.token );
    capability.allowClientIncoming( 'Admin' );
    capability.allowClientOutgoing( config.twilio.appid );
  var token = capability.generate();

    res.render('cc', {
        token:token,
        api_key:config.flybase.api_key,
        app_name:config.flybase.app_name
    });
});
```

```
app.get('/', function(req, res) {
    var client_name = "anonymous";
    if( typeof req.param("client") !== "undefined" ){
        client_name = req.param("client");
    }

    var capability = new twilio.Capability( config.twilio.
    sid, config.twilio.token );
    capability.allowClientIncoming( client_name );
    capability.allowClientOutgoing( config.twilio.appid );
  var token = capability.generate();

    res.render('index', {
        call_token: token,
        client_name: client_name
    });
});

var server = app.listen(port, function() {
    console.log('Listening on port %d', server.address().
    port);
});
```

The /cc and / routes both make calls to Twilio to create capability tokens for Twilio Client. These let the web page make and receive calls.

There was one thing we did to show tracking on the home page. If you access the page with a ?client=myname variable appended to it, then the name of the client changes. This is to demonstrate passing contextual information.

Setting Up Templates

We need to build our template files now. There will be two of them: **index.ejs** and **cc.ejs**. We will store them in the views folder.

First, let's set up **index.ejs**:

```HTML
<!DOCTYPE html>
<html>
<head>
    <title>Fly Shop</title>
    <link rel="stylesheet" href="//netdna.bootstrapcdn.com/
    bootstrap/3.1.0/css/bootstrap.min.css">
    <link href="//netdna.bootstrapcdn.com/font-awesome/4.0.3/
    css/font-awesome.min.css" rel="stylesheet">

    <script src="https://ajax.googleapis.com/ajax/libs/
    jquery/2.1.4/jquery.min.js"></script>
    <script type="text/javascript" src="//static.twilio.com/
    libs/twiliojs/1.2/twilio.min.js"></script>
    <script src="//netdna.bootstrapcdn.com/bootstrap/3.1.0/
    js/bootstrap.min.js"></script>
</head>
<body>
    <div class="container">
        <div class="row">
            <div class="col-md-6">
                <h1>Fly Shop</h1>
            </div>
        </div>
        <div class="well">
            <h4 class="text-center">Click an ad to
            purchase now!</h4>
```

```
</div>
<div class="row">
    <div class="col-md-4">
        <a onclick="call('Apple LCD TV');">
        <div class="panel panel-default">
            <div class="panel-heading">
            <h4>55" Apple LCD TV</h4></div>
            <div class="panel-body text-
            center">
                <img src="/images/apple1.
                png">
            </div>
        </div></a>
    </div>
    <div class="col-md-4">
        <a onclick="call('Apple iPad');">
        <div class="panel panel-default">
            <div class="panel-heading">
            <h4>Apple iPad</h4></div>
            <div class="panel-body text-
            center">
                <img src="/images/
                apple2.png">
            </div>
        </div></a>
    </div>
    <div class="col-md-4">
        <a onclick="call('MacBook Pro');">
        <div class="panel panel-default">
            <div class="panel-heading">
            <h4>MacBook Pro</h4></div>
```

```
                            <div class="panel-body
                            text-center">
                                    <img src="/images/apple6.
                                    png">
                            </div>
                    </div></a>
            </div>
        </div>
        <div class="well" style="display:none;"
        id="hangupbox">
                <a onClick="hangup();" class="btn
                btn-primary" id="hangup">Hang up</a>
        </div>
    </div>
    <script type="text/javascript">
        var myname = '';
        Twilio.Device.setup("<%=call_token%>");
        function call(item_of_choice) {
                params = {"item": item_of_choice, "name":
                "<%= client_name %>"};
                Twilio.Device.connect(params);
                $("#hangupbox").show();
        }
        function hangup() {
                Twilio.Device.disconnectAll();
                $("#hangupbox").hide();
        }
    </script>
</body>
</html>
```

This will display sample products and let a visitor click one. When they do, it will begin a call to the agent.

The images are in the "public/images" folder and are just some random product images. You can swap them out for any actual images you want to. This just gives you an idea how it works.

The actual workings of this page are in the JavaScript, which takes the modules **call_token** and **client_name** as well as the selected item the user is interested in talking about and begins a browser phone call.

Now, let's set up **cc.ejs**, which is the agent control panel:

```
<!DOCTYPE html>
<html>
<head>
    <title>Control Center</title>
    <link rel="stylesheet" href="//netdna.bootstrapcdn.com/
    bootstrap/3.1.0/css/bootstrap.min.css">
    <link href="//netdna.bootstrapcdn.com/font-awesome/4.0.3/
    css/font-awesome.min.css" rel="stylesheet">

    <script src="https://ajax.googleapis.com/ajax/libs/
    jquery/2.1.4/jquery.min.js"></script>
    <script type="text/javascript" src="//static.twilio.com/
    libs/twiliojs/1.2/twilio.min.js"></script>
</head>
<body>
    <div class="container">
        <div class="well">
            <h1>Incoming calls</h1>
        </div>
        <br />
        <div class="well">
            <div class="list-group">
                <div class="list-group-item">
```

```
                            <h4 class="list-group-item-
                            heading warning"></h4>
                    </div>
                </div>
            </div>
        </div>
    <script src="https://cdn.flybase.io/flybase.
    js?20150817"></script>
    <script>
        $(function(){
                var leadsRef = new Flybase( "<%= api_key %>",
                "<%= app_name %>", "leads");
                leadsRef.on("new-caller", function( call ) {
                        $('.warning').val( call.name + ' wants
                        a ' + call.item );
                });

                Twilio.Device.setup("<%= token %>");
                Twilio.Device.incoming(function (conn) {
                        // accept the incoming connection and
                            start two-way audio
                        conn.accept();
                });

                function hangup() {
                        Twilio.Device.disconnectAll();
                }
        });
    </script>
</body>
</html>
```

This will look a little like the "index" file. The difference is that it is for agents to view when a visitor clicks to begin a call. An alert will appear on the screen, and the call will be answered.

In our **app.js** file, we also set it up so that /cc was behind a basic password, so only agents can access it.

One last thing to do, let's fire up our app:

```
node app.js
```

We've told our app to run on port 5000, so if you go to your web browser and type in http://localhost:5000/, you should see your call center ad page, and if you go to http://localhost:5000/cc, you should see your actual call center, waiting for calls from site visitors. Clicking an ad from the home page will trigger a call with the call center.

If you're running this locally, you'll want to make sure you've got *ngrok* running before you go to the next step. If you haven't used ngrok (https://ngrok.com/) before, Kevin Whinnery over at Twilio has put together a great tutorial (www.twilio.com/blog/2013/10/test-your-webhooks-locally-with-ngrok.html) to help you get started.

Summary

We've built a real-time click-to-call call center app using Flybase (http://flybase.io) and Twilio (http://twilio.com). This is a very basic implementation, designed to show you the possibilities of a real-time "click-to-call" service using Twilio Client and Flybase. You can use this project and the open source code (https://github.com/flybaseio/call-ads) to extend the tutorial and begin building your own applications.

Here are some ideas to get your brain juices flowing on how you could use real-time information like this with "click to call":

- Bring up caller information as the call is made to speed up calls.

- Gather location data from callers to automatically geographically place them.

- Allow for multiple agents. Maybe even look into using Flybase to store incoming call queues and connecting the customer to the first available agent.

CHAPTER 5

Building a Salesforce-Powered Call Center

In the world of telephony, an automated call distribution (ACD) system is a system that distributes incoming calls to a specific group of agents based on the customer's selection, customer's telephone number, selected incoming line to the system, or time of day the call was processed. We also call this a call center.

A couple years ago, Twilio's Charles Oppenheimer (`https://github.com/choppen5`) built a demo of a Salesforce-embeddable ACD (`https://github.com/choppen5/client-acd`) using Twilio Client and Ruby. Much credit to Charles in this regard.

We have simply taken Charles' demo and converted it to Node.js with a Flybase-powered backend to handle the distribution of calls, rather than the original Ruby/Mongo system. The result is a cleaner call center that's easy to modify and integrate into other CRMs.

Necessary Tools

- Flybase.io (`https://flybase.io/`) as our backend, handling storing data, passing events, and our call queues.

© Roger Stringer 2021
R. Stringer, *Real-Time Twilio and Flybase*, https://doi.org/10.1007/978-1-4842-7074-5_5

- Twilio Client (www.twilio.com/webrtc), a WebRTC interface to Twilio. In our demo, we are using the JavaScript library that gives us an API and connection to Twilio to receive the call within our Salesforce browser delivering the call via WebRTC. Twilio Client also gives us the ability to control the call via our softphone.

- Heroku will be used as our web host, but you can host your call center anywhere you'd like.

- Salesforce Open CTI (https://developer. salesforce.com/page/Open_CTI) is an open API to allow third-party CTI vendors to connect telephony channels into the Salesforce CRM interface. In our demo, we use Open CTI to house our softphone and drive the click-to-dial/text functionality. The demo requires no plugins or installed software, thanks to the design of Open CTI.

The actual Salesforce integration is optional, and you can easily insert your softphone into another CRM. Part 2 of this tutorial will actually use Flybase to build a simple CRM with the softphone included as a widget.

Getting Started

You can find the full source code here: https://github.com/flybaseio/callcenter.

First, let's set up our Node.js app.

Create "package.json":

```json
{

  "name": "callcenter",
  "version": "0.0.1",
  "description": "Client ACD powered by Flybase, Twilio and
                 Node.js",
  "main": "app.js",
  "repository": "https://github.com/flybaseio/callcenter",
  "scripts": {
    "test": "echo \"Error: no test specified\" && exit 1"
  },
  "keywords": [
    "twilio",
    "data mcfly",
    "flybase",
    "twilio",
    "sms"
  ],
  "author": "Roger Stringer",
  "license": "MIT",
  "dependencies": {
    "body-parser": "~1.4.2",
    "ejs": "~0.8.5",
    "express": "~3.4.8",
    "flybase": "1.7.2",
    "less-middleware": "~0.2.1-beta",
    "method-override": "~2.0.2",
    "moment": "~2.5.1",
    "node-buzz": "~1.1.0",
    "twilio": "~1.6.0"
  },
```

```
  "engines": {
    "node": "0.12"
  }
}
```

This will tell our call center what modules we want to install for our Node app. Now, we want to create our "app.js" file to handle all our backend work:

```
var express = require('express');
var bodyParser = require('body-parser');
var methodOverride = require('method-override');
var path = require('path');

var config = require( path.join(__dirname, 'app', 'config') );

var app = express();
app.set('views', path.join(__dirname, 'app', 'views'));
app.engine('html', require('ejs').renderFile);
app.set('view engine', 'html');
app.use(bodyParser.json());
app.use(bodyParser.urlencoded({     extended: true     }));
app.use(express.static( path.join(__dirname, 'app', 'public')));

var port = process.env.PORT || 5000; // set our port

var twilio = require('twilio');
var client = twilio(config.twilio.sid, config.twilio.token);

var flybase = require('flybase');
var callsRef = flybase.init(config.flybase.app_name, "calls",
                config.flybase.api_key);
```

```
var agentsRef = flybase.init(config.flybase.app_name, "agents",
config.flybase.api_key);
var queueId = '';
var good2go = false;

// backend routes

client.queues.list(function(err, data) {
    var to_go = data.queues.length;
    data.queues.forEach(function(queue) {
        if( queue.friendlyName === config.twilio.queueName ){
            queueId = queue.sid;
            console.log( "Queueid = #" + queueId +
            " for #" +  config.twilio.queueName );
            good2go = true;
        }
        to_go--;
        if( to_go == 0 ){
            if( queueId === '' ){
                client.queues.create({
                    friendlyName: config.twilio.queueName
                }, function(err, queue) {
                    queueId = queue.sid;
                });
            }
        }
    });
});

// listen for events via Flybase...
// if an agent gets disconnected then we log them off...
agentsRef.on('agent-removed', function (data) {
    var data = JSON.parse( data );
```

```
        console.log( data.username + " has left the building");
        update_agent(data.username,{
            status: 'LoggedOut'
        });
});

// return number of agents with status set to Ready
agentsRef.on('get-ready-agents', function (data) {
    var adNag = function() {
        agentsRef.where({"status": 'Ready'}).
        on('value',function( rec ){
            console.log( rec.count() + ' agents are Ready' );
            if( rec.count() ){
                agentsRef.trigger('agents-ready', rec.
                count() );
            }else{
                agentsRef.trigger('agents-ready', "0" );
            }
        });
    };
    setTimeout(adNag, 1500);
});

//     listen for outgoing calls
app.post('/dial', function (req, res) {
    var phoneNumber = req.param('PhoneNumber');
    var dial_id = config.twilio.fromNumber;
    if( typeof req.param('CallerID') !== 'undefined' ){
        var dial_id = req.param('CallerID');
    }
```

```
    var twiml = new twilio.TwimlResponse();
    twiml.dial(phoneNumber, {
        callerId:dial_id
    });
    console.log("Response text for /dial post = #", twiml.
    toString());
    res.writeHead(200, {
        'Content-Type':'text/xml'
    });
    res.end( twiml.toString() );
});

//     listen for incoming calls
app.post('/voice', function (req, res) {
    var queuename = config.twilio.queueName;
    var sid = req.param('CallSid');
    var callerId = req.param('Caller');

    var addToQ = 0;
    var dialQueue = '';
    var client_name = '';

    //     searches for an agent who has been set to Ready for
           the longest time and connects them to the caller...
    getLongestIdle(true, function( bestClient ){
        if( bestClient ){
            console.log("Routing incoming voice call to best
            agent = #", bestClient);
            var client_name = bestClient;
```

```
    }else{
        console.log( 'no agent was found, adding caller
        to #', config.twilio.queueName );
        var dialQueue = queuename;
        addToQ = 1;
    }

    var twiml = new twilio.TwimlResponse();
    if( addToQ ){
        twiml.say("Please wait for the next available
        agent",{
            voice:'woman'
        }).enqueue(config.twilio.queueName);
    }else{
        twiml.dial({
            'timeout':'10',
            'action':'/handledialcallstatus',
            'callerId':callerid
        }, function(node) {
            this.client( client_name );
        });
        update_call(sid, {
            'sid': sid,
            'agent': client_name,
            'status': 'ringing'
        });
    }
    console.log("Response text for /voice post = #",
    twiml.toString());
```

```
        res.writeHead(200, {
            'Content-Type':'text/xml'
        });
        res.end( twiml.toString() );
    });
});

app.post('/handledialcallstatus', function (req, res) {
    var sid = req.param('CallSid');
    var twiml = new twilio.TwimlResponse();

    if( req.param('DialCallStatus') == 'no-answer' ){
        callsRef.where({"sid": sid}).on('value',function( rec ){
            if( rec.count() !== null ){
                var sidinfo = rec.first().value();
                if( sidinfo ){
                    var agent = sidinfo.agent;
                    update_agent(agent, {
                        'status': 'missed'
                    });
                }
                // Change agent status for agents that
                   missed calls
            }
            //      redirect and try to get a new agent...
            twiml.redirect('/voice');
        });
    }else{
        twiml.hangup();
    }
    console.log("Response text for /handledialcallstatus
    post = #", twiml.toString());
```

```javascript
    res.writeHead(200, {
        'Content-Type':'text/xml'
    });
    res.end( twiml.toString() );
});

// assign a twilio call token to the agent
app.get('/token', function(req, res) {
    var client_name = "anonymous";
    if( typeof req.param("client") !== "undefined" ){
        client_name = req.param("client");
    }

    var capability = new twilio.Capability( config.twilio.sid,
    config.twilio.token );
    capability.allowClientIncoming( client_name );
    capability.allowClientOutgoing( config.twilio.appid );
    var token = capability.generate();

    res.end(token);
});

// return flybase info to the softphone...
app.get('/getconfig', function(req, res) {
    res.json({
        app_name: config.flybase.app_name,
        api_key: config.flybase.api_key
    });
});

// return a phone number
app.get('/getCallerId', function(req, res) {
    var client_name = "anonymous";
    if( typeof req.param("from") !== "undefined" ){
```

```
            client_name = req.param("from");
        }
        res.end( config.twilio.fromNumber );
});

app.post('/track', function(req, res) {

});

app.get('/', function(req, res) {
        var client_name = "anonymous";
        if( typeof req.param("client") !== "undefined" ){
            client_name = req.param("client");
        }

        res.render('index', {
            client_name: client_name,
            anyCallerId: 'none'
        });
});

var server = app.listen(port, function() {
        console.log('Listening on port %d', server.address().
        port);
});
// various functions ==========================================

//      find the caller who's been `Ready` the longest
function getLongestIdle( callRouting, callback ){
        if( callRouting ){
            agentsRef.where({"status": "DeQueuing"}).orderBy(
            {"readytime":-1} ).on('value').then(function( data ){
                var agent = data.first().value();
                callback( agent.client );
```

```
            },function(err){
                agentsRef.where({"status": "Ready"}).orderBy
                ( {"readytime":-1} ).on('value').then(function
                ( data ){
                    var agent = data.first().value();
                    callback( agent.client );
                },function(err){
                    callback( false );
                });
            });
        }else{
            agentsRef.where({"status": "Ready"}).orderBy(
            {"readytime":-1} ).on('value').then(function( data ){
                var agent = data.first().value();
                callback( agent.client );
            },function(err){
                callback( false );
            });
        }
}

// check if the user exists and if they do then we update,
   otherwise we insert...
function update_agent(client, data, cb){
    var d = new Date();
    var date = d.toLocaleString();
    var callback = cb || null;
    agentsRef.where({"client": client}).once('value').then(
    function( rec ){
        var agent = rec.first().value();
        for( var i in data ){
            agent[i] = data[i];
```

```
        }
        agentsRef.push(agent, function(resp) {
            console.log( "agent updated" );
            if( callback !== null ){
                callback();
            }
        });
    },function(err){
        data.client = client;
        agentsRef.push(data, function(resp) {
            console.log( "agent inserted" );
            if( callback !== null ){
                callback();
            }
        });
    });
}

function update_call(sid, data){
    var d = new Date();
    var date = d.toLocaleString();
    callsRef.where({"sid": sid}).on('value').then( function(
    rec ){
        var call = rec.first().value();
        for( var i in data ){
            call[i] = data[i];
        }
        callsRef.push(call, function(resp) {
            console.log( "call updated" );
        });
```

```
    },function(err){
        data.sid = sid;
        callsRef.push(data, function(resp) {
            console.log( "call inserted" );
        });
    });
}

// call queue handling

var qSum = 0;
var checkQueue = function() {
    qSum += 1;
    var qSize = 0;
    var readyAgents = 0;
    var qname = config.twilio.queueName;
    client.queues(queueId).get(function(err, queue) {
        qSize = queue.currentSize;
        console.log( 'There are #' + qSize + ' callers in the
        queue (' + queueId + ')' );
        if( qSize > 0 ){
            agentsRef.where({"status": "Ready"}).orderBy
            ( {"readytime":-1} ).on('value').then(function
            ( agents ){
                var readyAgents = agents.count();
                var bestClient = agents.first().value();
                console.log("Found best client - routing
                to #" + bestClient.client + " - setting
                agent to DeQueuing status so they aren't
                sent another call from the queue");
                update_agent(bestClient.client, {status:
                "DeQueuing" }, function(){
```

```
                    console.log('redirecting call now!');
                    client.queues(queueId).
                    members("Front").update({
                            url: config.twilio.dqueueurl,
                            method: "POST"
                    }, function(err, member) {
//                              console.log(member.
                                position);
                    });
                });
            },function(err){
                console.log("No Ready agents during queue
                poll #" + qSum);
            });
            agentsRef.trigger('agents-ready', readyAgents );
            agentsRef.trigger('in-queue', qSize );

            // restart the check checking
            setTimeout(checkQueue, 3000);
        }else{
            // restart the check checking
            console.log("No callers found during queue
            poll #" + qSum);
            setTimeout(checkQueue, 3000);
        }
    });
};
setTimeout(checkQueue, 1500);
```

Recapping the Code

There's a lot happening in this file. First, we require our various libraries and set up express. Then we start our actual work.

You'll notice we set up two Flybase references:

> - callsRef connects to our **calls** table and handles storing and retrieving information for incoming calls.

> - agentsRef connects to our agents table and handles storing and retrieving information for agents.

The first backend task we handle is checking our Twilio queues to retrieve the **queueId** or our call queue, or else create it if it doesn't exist. We use this queue for storing incoming calls if there are no agents available in our call center, and they stay inside the queue until an agent is available.

Then we set up event listeners for two events:

> - agent-removed: When an agent logs out, then we update their user record to set them to not ready.

> - get-ready-agents: Just returns the number of agents currently set to Ready.

Then we have our actual URI endpoints:

> - /dial is a POST request that is handled by Twilio to make outgoing calls between the agent's web browser and a phone number.

> - /voice is a POST request that handles incoming calls from phone numbers. This works by finding the agent that has had their status set to Ready for the

longest time and assigning them to the call. If the agent is not Ready, then we place the caller in a queue and check it later.

- /**handDialCallStatus** is a POST request that is called when a call finishes. It checks to see if the call was answered or not answered and, depending on the DialCallStatus returned from Twilio, either places the caller back into the queue and takes the agent out of the Ready status or hangs up the call as it assumes the call is done.

- /token is a GET request called via an AJAX call on the frontend to assign a Twilio Client capability token to the agent while they are logged in.

- /getconfig is a GET request called also via an AJAX call from the client that returns the call center's Flybase settings for the softphone to use in the frontend.

- / is a GET request that displays the softphone and assigns a name to the client based on the ?client query string.

We have three backbone functions that are used by the call center to handle various purposes:

- **getLongestIdle** is a function that checks for either an agent whose status is set to Ready or "*DeQueuing*" and returns that agent's client name. In the case of no agents being found, then we return false, and it places the caller in the queue. "DeQueuing" is a special status we'll be setting at the end of our code as an agent becomes available.

> - **update_agent** will take the agent's ID and update
> their account in the Flybase database with new info,
> such as status updates when on a call, going offline, etc.
>
> - **update_call** is used in the same way as update_
> agent but for tracking calls.

Finally, we have the queue handling function called **checkQueue**, which is called 1.5 seconds after the app loads and then performs a simple task every 3 seconds:

1. It enters into a loop to return all callers in the call queue.

2. If there are callers waiting to connect to agents, then it will look for the agent with their status set to Ready and who has been Ready the longest by sorting by the readyTime field.

3. If an agent is Ready, then we set that agent's status to DeQueuing and connect the caller at the Front of the queue to that agent by calling our dqueueurl.

4. If no agents are Ready or no callers are in the queue, then we set a timeout to call the function again in 3 seconds and return to step 1 of the "checkQueue" loop.

We next want to create a folder called "app" and then inside that folder create a file called config.js:

```
module.exports = {
    // Twilio API keys
    twilio: {
        sid: "ACCOUNT-SID",
        token: "AUTH-TOKEN",
        appid: 'APP-ID',
```

```
        fromNumber : "TWILIO-NUMBER",
        welcome : "Thank you for calling.",
        hangup : false,
        queueName: "cnacd",
        dqueueurl:"http://yourwebsite.com/voice"
    },
    //    Flybase settings
    flybase: {
        api_key: "YOUR-API-KEY",
        app_name: "YOUR-FLYBASE-APP"
    }
};
```

Update this file to contain your Twilio information and your Flybase information.

For the Twilio information, you'll need to create a TwiML app inside your Twilio account. Create the app and have it POST to your call center website at /dial.

Also, create a new phone number inside Twilio and have that phone number POST to your call center website at /voice.

There is a variable called queueName, which is the name of the queue you want your call center to use, and also a variable called dqueueurl, which is the URL to your website with /voice appended to it. You will need this for the dequeuing task as Twilio requires an absolute URL.

The Softphone

Inside the app folder, create two folders:

1. views

2. public

Inside "public," create a file called "index.html":

```html
<!DOCTYPE html>
<html>
<head>
    <title>Twilio Softphone</title>
    <script type="text/javascript" src="https://static.twilio.
    com/libs/twiliojs/1.2/twilio.min.js"></script>
    <script src="https://ajax.googleapis.com/ajax/libs/
    jquery/2.2.0/jquery.min.js"></script>
    <script src="https://na15.salesforce.com/support/api/31.0/
    interaction.js"></script>
    <script src="https://na15.salesforce.com/support/
    console/31.0/integration.js"></script>
    <script src="https://cdn.flybase.io/flybase.js"></script>
    <script type="text/javascript" src="/js/softphone.js">
    </script>
    <link rel="stylesheet" type="text/css" href="/css/dialer.css">
</head>
<body>
    <div id="client_name" hidden="true"><%= client_name %>
    </div>
    <div id="softphone" class="softphone">
        <div id="agent-status-controls" class="clearfix">
            <button class="agent-status ready">Ready
            </button>
            <button class="agent-status not-ready">Not Ready
            </button>
            <div class="agent-status active">Call In-
            Progress</div>
        </div><!-- /agent-status -->
```

```html
<div id="agent-status">
    <p></p>
</div> /agent-status -->

<div class="divider"></div>

<div id="number-entry">
    <input placeholder="+1 (555) 555-5555"></input>
    <div class="incoming-call-status">Incoming
    Call</div>
</div><!-- /number-entry -->

<div id="dialer">
    <div id="dialer-container">
        <div class="numpad-container">
            <div class="number" value="1">1</div>
            <div class="number" value="2">2</div>
            <div class="number" value="3">3</div>
            <div class="number" value="4">4</div>
            <div class="number" value="5">5</div>
            <div class="number" value="6">6</div>
            <div class="number" value="7">7</div>
            <div class="number" value="8">8</div>
            <div class="number" value="9">9</div>
            <div class="number ast" value="*">
            &lowast;</div><div class="number"
            value="0">0</div><div class="number"
            value="#">#</div>
        </div> /numpad-container -->
    </div><!-- /dialer-container -->
</div><!-- /dialer -->
```

```
<div id="action-button-container">
    <div id="action-buttons">
        <button class="call">Call</button>
        <button class="answer">Answer</button>
        <button class="hangup">Hangup</button>
        <button class="mute">Mute</button>
        <button class="hold">Hold</button>
        <button class="unhold">UnHold</button>
    </div><!-- /action-buttons -->
</div><!---action-button-container -->

<div id="call-data">
    <h3>Caller info</h3>
    <ul class="name"><strong>Name: </strong><span
    class="caller-name"></span></ul>
    <ul class="phone_number"><strong>Number:
    </strong><span class="caller-number"></span></ul>
    <ul class="queue"><strong>Queue: </strong><span
    class="caller-queue"></span></ul>
    <ul class="message"><strong>Message:
    </strong><span class="caller-message"></span></ul>
</div><!-- /call-data -->

<div id="callerid-entry" style="display:
<%= anycallerid %>">
    <input placeholder="Change your Caller ID ">
    </input>
</div><!-- /number-entry -->

<div id="team-status">
    <div class="agents-status"><div class="agents-
    num">-</div>Agents</div>
```

```
            <div class="queues-status"><div class="queues-
            num">-</div>In-Queue</div>
        </div><!-- /team-status -->
    </div><!-- /softphone -->
</body>
</html>
```

This is our index file, which handles the output of our softphone for agents to use to accept and make calls.

Inside the public folder, create a folder called "css" and include the following two files :

"dialer.css":

```
/* reset css */
article,aside,details,figcaption,figure,footer,header,hgroup,
hr,menu,nav,section{display:block}a,hr{padding:0}abbr,address,
article,aside,audio,b,blockquote,body,canvas,caption,cite,code,
dd,del,details,dfn,div,dl,dt,em,fieldset,figcaption,figure,
footer,form,h1,h2,h3,h4,h5,h6,header,hgroup,html,i,iframe,img,
ins,kbd,label,legend,li,mark,menu,nav,object,ol,p,pre,q,samp,
section,small,span,strong,sub,summary,sup,table,tbody,td,tfoot,
th,thead,time,tr,ul,var,video{margin:0;padding:0;border:0;out
line:0;font-size:100%;vertical-align:baseline;background:0 0}
ins,mark{background-color:#ff9;color:#000}body{line-height:1}
nav ul{list-style:none}blockquote,q{quotes:none}blockquote:
after,blockquote:before,q:after,q:before{content:'';content:
none}a{margin:0;font-size:100%;vertical-align:baseline;
background:0 0}ins{text-decoration:none}mark{font-style:
italic;font-weight:700}del{text-decoration:line-through}
abbr[title],dfn[title]{border-bottom:1px dotted;cursor:help}
table{border-collapse:collapse;border-spacing:0}
hr{height:1px;border:0;border-top:1px solid #ccc;margin:1em 0}
input,select{vertical-align:middle}
```

```css
.clearfix:before, .clearfix:after { content: " "; display:
table; }
.clearfix:after { clear: both; }
.clearfix { *zoom: 1; }

*, *:before, *:after {
  -moz-box-sizing: border-box; -webkit-box-sizing: border-box;
  box-sizing: border-box;
  -webkit-touch-callout: none;
  -webkit-user-select: none;
  -khtml-user-select: none;
  -moz-user-select: none;
  -ms-user-select: none;
  user-select: none;
}

body {
  font-family: "Helvetica", Arial, sans-serif;
  background-color: white;
}

#softphone {
  width: 175px;
  margin: 10px auto 0px;
}

#agent-status-controls {
  margin: 10px 0 20px;
  position: relative;
}

.agent-status {
  border: none;
  padding: 6px 10px;
```

```
  background-image: linear-gradient(bottom, #ddd 20%, #eee 72%);
  background-image: -o-linear-gradient(bottom, #ddd 20%, #eee 72%);
  background-image: -moz-linear-gradient(bottom, #ddd 20%,
               #eee 72%);
  background-image: -webkit-linear-gradient(bottom, #ddd 20%,
               #eee 72%);
  background-image: -ms-linear-gradient(bottom, #ddd 20%, #eee 72%);
  background-image: -webkit-gradient(linear, left bottom,
               left top, color-stop(0.2, #ddd), color-
               stop(0.72, #eee));
  color: #333;
  text-shadow: 0px -1px 0px rgba(255, 255, 255, 0.3);
  box-shadow: inset 0px 0px 1px rgba(0, 0, 0, 0.4);
  cursor: pointer;
  text-align: center;
}

button.agent-status {
  display: inline-block;
  float: left;
  width: 50%;
  margin: 0;
  -webkit-appearance: none;
  -moz-appearance: none;
  appearance: none;
}

@-webkit-keyframes pulse {
  0% {background-color: #EA6045;}
  50% {background-color: #e54a23;}
  100% {background-color: #EA6045;}
}
```

```
div.agent-status {
  position: absolute;
  top: 0;
  left: 0;
  width: 100%;
  height: 100%;
  z-index: 1000;
  font-size: 12px;
  line-height: 12px;
  background-image: none;
  background-color: #EA6045;
  -webkit-animation: pulse 1s infinite alternate;
  color: #fff;
  text-shadow: 0px -1px 0px rgba(0, 0, 0, 0.2);
  border-radius: 2px;
}

.agent-status:active, .agent-status:focus {
  outline: none;
}

.agent-status[disabled] {
  box-shadow: inset 0px 0px 15px rgba(0, 0, 0, 0.6);
  opacity: 0.8;
  text-shadow: 0px 1px 0px rgba(0, 0, 0, 0.4);
}

.agent-status.ready {
  border-radius: 2px 0 0 2px;
}
```

```
.agent-status.ready[disabled] {
  background-image: linear-gradient(bottom, #7eac20 20%,
                    #91c500 72%);
  background-image: -o-linear-gradient(bottom, #7eac20 20%,
                    #91c500 72%);
  background-image: -moz-linear-gradient(bottom, #7eac20 20%,
                    #91c500 72%);
  background-image: -webkit-linear-gradient(bottom, #7eac20
                    20%, #91c500 72%);
  background-image: -ms-linear-gradient(bottom, #7eac20 20%,
                    #91c500 72%);
  background-image: -webkit-gradient(linear, left bottom, left
                    top, color-stop(0.2, #7eac20), color-stop
                    (0.72, #91c500));
  color: #f5f5f5;
}

.agent-status.not-ready {
  border-radius: 0 2px 2px 0;
}

.agent-status.not-ready[disabled] {
  background-image: linear-gradient(bottom, #e64118 20%,
                    #e54a23 72%);
  background-image: -o-linear-gradient(bottom, #e64118 20%,
                    #e54a23 72%);
  background-image: -moz-linear-gradient(bottom, #e64118 20%,
                    #e54a23 72%);
  background-image: -webkit-linear-gradient(bottom, #e64118
                    20%, #e54a23 72%);
  background-image: -ms-linear-gradient(bottom, #e64118 20%,
                    #e54a23 72%);
```

```css
  background-image: -webkit-gradient(linear, left bottom, left
                    top, color-stop(0.2, #e64118), color-stop
                    (0.72, #e54a23));
  color: #f5f5f5;
}

#dialer {
  border: solid 1px #ddd;
  border-width: 0 0 0 1px;
  -webkit-transition: opacity 1s;
  transition: opacity 1s;
}

input {
  border: solid 1px #ddd;
  border-bottom-color: #d5d5d5;
  border-radius: 2px 2px 0 0;
  font-size: 16px;
  width: 100%;
  padding: 14px 5px;
  display: block;
  text-align: center;
  margin: 0;
  position: relative;
  z-index: 100;
  -webkit-transition: border-color 1s;
  transition: border-color 1s;
}

#number-entry {
  position: relative;
  height: 48px;
}
```

```css
.incoming input {
  border: solid 1px red;
}

.incoming #dialer {
  opacity: 0.25;
}

.softphone .incoming-call-status {
  position: absolute;
  display: none;
  top: 100%;
  left: 0;
  right: 0;
  background: red;
  color: #fff;
  font-size: 16px;
  padding: 6px 0;
  text-align: center;
  width: 100%;
  z-index: 200;
  border-radius: 0 0 2px 2px;
  opacity: 0;
  -webkit-transition: opacity 1s;
  transition: opacity 1s;
}

.incoming .incoming-call-status {
  display: block;
  opacity: 1;
}
```

```css
.number {
  color: #555;
  font-weight: 300;
  cursor: pointer;
  display: inline-block;
  height: 38px;
  line-height: 38px;
  font-size: 21px;
  width: 33.333333333%;
  background-image: linear-gradient(bottom, #e9e9e9 20%,
                    #e5e5e5 72%);
  background-image: -o-linear-gradient(bottom, #e9e9e9 20%,
                    #e5e5e5 72%);
  background-image: -moz-linear-gradient(bottom, #e9e9e9 20%,
                    #e5e5e5 72%);
  background-image: -webkit-linear-gradient(bottom, #e9e9e9
                    20%, #e5e5e5 72%);
  background-image: -ms-linear-gradient(bottom, #e9e9e9 20%,
                    #e5e5e5 72%);
  background-image: -webkit-gradient(linear, left bottom,
                    left top, color-stop(0.2, #e9e9e9),
                    color-stop(0.72, #e5e5e5));
  text-shadow: 0px 1px 0px #f5f5f5;
  filter: dropshadow(color=#f5f5f5, offx=0, offy=1);
  text-align: center;
  box-shadow: inset 1px 0px 0px rgba(255, 255, 255, 0.4),
    inset -1px 0px 0px rgba(0, 0, 0, 0.1),
    inset 0px 1px 0px #f5f5f5,
    inset 0 -1px 0px #d6d6d6;
}
```

```css
.number.ast {
  font-size: 33px;
  line-height: 32px;
  vertical-align: -1px;
}

.number:hover {
  background-image: linear-gradient(bottom, #f5f5f5 20%,
                    #f0f0f0 72%);
  background-image: -o-linear-gradient(bottom, #f5f5f5 20%,
                    #f0f0f0 72%);
  background-image: -moz-linear-gradient(bottom, #f5f5f5 20%,
                    #f0f0f0 72%);
  background-image: -webkit-linear-gradient(bottom, #f5f5f5
                    20%, #f0f0f0 72%);
  background-image: -ms-linear-gradient(bottom, #f5f5f5 20%,
                    #f0f0f0 72%);
  background-image: -webkit-gradient(linear, left bottom, left
                    top, color-stop(0.2, #f5f5f5), color-stop
                    (0.72, #f0f0f0));
}

.number:active {
  box-shadow: inset 1px 0px 0px rgba(255, 255, 255, 0.4),
    inset -1px 0px 0px rgba(0, 0, 0, 0.1),
    inset 0px 1px 0px #f5f5f5,
    inset 0 -1px 0px #d6d6d6,
    inset 0px 0px 5px 2px rgba(0, 0, 0, 0.15);
}

#action-buttons button {
  -webkit-appearance: none;
  -moz-appearance: none;
```

```
  appearance: none;
  display: inline-block;
  border: none;
  margin: 0;
  cursor: pointer;
}

#action-buttons .call {
  color: #f5f5f5;
  width: 100%;
  font-size: 18px;
  padding: 8px 0;
  text-shadow: 0px -1px 0px rgba(0, 0, 0, 0.3);
  margin: 0;
  background-image: linear-gradient(bottom, #7eac20 20%,
                    #91c500 72%);
  background-image: -o-linear-gradient(bottom, #7eac20 20%,
                    #91c500 72%);
  background-image: -moz-linear-gradient(bottom, #7eac20 20%,
                    #91c500 72%);
  background-image: -webkit-linear-gradient(bottom, #7eac20
                    20%, #91c500 72%);
  background-image: -ms-linear-gradient(bottom, #7eac20 20%,
                    #91c500 72%);
  background-image: -webkit-gradient(linear, left bottom,
                    left top, color-stop(0.2, #7eac20),
                    color-stop(0.72, #91c500));
  border-radius: 0 0 2px 2px;
}

#action-buttons .answer, #action-buttons .hangup {
  color: #f5f5f5;
  width: 100%;
```

```
  font-size: 18px;
  padding: 8px 0;
  text-shadow: 0px -1px 0px rgba(0, 0, 0, 0.4);
  margin: 0;
  background-image: linear-gradient(bottom, #e64118 20%,
                    #e54a23 72%);
  background-image: -o-linear-gradient(bottom, #e64118 20%,
                    #e54a23 72%);
  background-image: -moz-linear-gradient(bottom, #e64118 20%,
                    #e54a23 72%);
  background-image: -webkit-linear-gradient(bottom, #e64118
                    20%, #e54a23 72%);
  background-image: -ms-linear-gradient(bottom, #e64118 20%,
                    #e54a23 72%);
  background-image: -webkit-gradient(linear, left bottom,
                    left top, color-stop(0.2, #e64118),
                    color-stop(0.72, #e54a23));
  border-radius: 0 0 2px 2px;
}

#action-buttons .hold, #action-buttons .unhold, #action-buttons
.mute {
  color: #444;
  width: 50%;
  font-size: 14px;
  padding: 12px 0;
  text-shadow: 0px 1px 0px rgba(255, 255, 255, 0.3);
  margin: 0;
  background-image: linear-gradient(bottom, #bbb 20%, #ccc 72%);
  background-image: -o-linear-gradient(bottom, #bbb 20%,
                    #ccc 72%);
```

```
  background-image: -moz-linear-gradient(bottom, #bbb 20%,
                    #ccc 72%);
  background-image: -webkit-linear-gradient(bottom, #bbb 20%,
                    #ccc 72%);
  background-image: -ms-linear-gradient(bottom, #bbb 20%,
                    #ccc 72%);
  background-image: -webkit-gradient(linear, left bottom,
                    left top, color-stop(0.2, #bbb),
                    color-stop(0.72, #ccc));
  box-shadow: inset 1px 0px 0px rgba(255, 255, 255, 0.4),
    inset -1px 0px 0px rgba(0, 0, 0, 0.1);
}

.mute {
  border-radius: 0 0 0 2px;
}

.hold, .unhold {
  border-radius: 0 2px 0 0;
}

#team-status .agents-status, #team-status .queues-status {
  display: inline-block;
  width: 45%;
  margin: 0;
  font-size: 14px;
  text-align: center;
  padding: 12px 0 16px;
  border-bottom: solid 1px #e5e5e5;
}

#team-status [class*="num"] {
  font-size: 32px;
```

```css
  font-weight: bold;
  margin-bottom: 6px;
}

#call-data {
  display: none;
}

.powered-by {
  text-align: right;
  padding: 10px 0;
}

img {
  width: 100px;
}
```

Finally, we want to set up our softphone frontend code.

Softphone Frontend Code

Create a folder inside public called js and add softphone.js.

This code is based on the original softphone.js code that Charles wrote, but I've added in Flybase queries directly to the frontend and then set up event listeners:

```javascript
$(function() {
    // ** Application container ** //
    window.SP = {}

    // Global state
    SP.state = {};
    SP.agentsRef = {};
```

```
SP.callsRef = {};
SP.agent = {};
SP.state.callNumber = null;
SP.state.calltype = "";
SP.username = $('#client_name').text();
SP.currentCall = null;      //instance variable for
                                tracking current connection
SP.requestedHold = false; //set if agent requested hold
                                button

SP.functions = {};

// Get a Twilio Client name and register with Twilio
SP.functions.getTwilioClientName = function(sfdcResponse) {
    sforce.interaction.runApex('UserInfo', 'getUserName', '' ,
    SP.functions.registerTwilioClient);
}

SP.functions.registerTwilioClient = function(response) {
    console.log("Registering with client name: " +
    response.result);
    // Twilio does not accept special characters in
       Client names
    var useresult = response.result;
    useresult = useresult.replace("@", "AT");
    useresult = useresult.replace(".", "DOT");
    SP.username = useresult;
    console.log("useresult = " + useresult);

    $.get("/getconfig", {"client":SP.username},
    function (data) {
        if( typeof data.api_key !== 'undefined' ){
            // agents...
```

```
        SP.agentsRef = new Flybase( data.api_key,
        data.app_name, 'agents');
        SP.agentsRef.isReady( function(){
            SP.functions.startWebSocket();
        });
        // calls...
        SP.callsRef = new Flybase( data.api_key,
        data.app_name, 'calls');
    }else{
        console.log( "umm yeah, something's broken.
        Please fix it");
    }
});

$.get("/token", {"client":SP.username}, function
(token) {
    Twilio.Device.setup(token, {debug: true});
});

$.get("/getCallerId", { "from":SP.username},
function(data) {
    $("#callerid-entry > input").val(data);
});

}

SP.functions.startWebSocket = function() {
    // ** Agent Presence Stuff ** //
    console.log(".startWebSocket...");
    var d = new Date();
    var date = d.toLocaleString();
//      look up or add agent:
    SP.functions.update_agent(SP.username,{
```

```
                status: 'LoggingIn',
                readytime: date
        });
        SP.agentsRef.on('agents-ready', function (data) {
                $("#team-status .agents-num").text( data );
        });
        SP.agentsRef.on('in-queue', function (data) {
                $("#team-status .queues-num").text( data);
        });

        SP.agentsRef.onDisconnect( function(){
                // if the agent gets disconnected for any
                    reason, then we want to kick them offline...
                SP.agentsRef.trigger('agent-removed',{username:
                SP.username});
        });
    }

//      update or insert agent.. don't keep re-adding the same
        agent..
    SP.functions.update_agent = function(client, data){
        var d = new Date();
        var date = d.toLocaleString();
        SP.agentsRef.where({"client": client}).once('value').
        then(function( rec ){
            var agent = rec.first().value();
            for( var i in data ){
                agent[i] = data[i];
            }
            SP.agent = agent;
            SP.agentsRef.push(agent, function(resp) {
                console.log( "agent updated" );
            });
```

```
    }, function(err){
        data.client = client;
        SP.agent = data;
        SP.agentsRef.push(data, function(resp) {
            console.log( "agent inserted" );
        });
    });
}

// ** UI Widgets ** //

// Hook up numpad to input field
$("div.number").bind('click',function(){
    //$("#number-entry > input").val($("#number-entry >
    input").val()+$(this).attr('Value'));
    //pass key without conn to a function
    SP.functions.handleKeyEntry($(this).attr('Value'));

});

SP.functions.handleKeyEntry = function (key) {
    if (SP.currentCall != null) {
        console.log("sending DTMF" + key);
        SP.currentCall.sendDigits(key);
    } else {
        $("#number-entry > input").val($("#number-entry
        > input").val()+key);
    }

}

//called when agent is not on a call
SP.functions.setIdleState = function() {
    $("#action-buttons > .call").show();
```

```
        $("#action-buttons > .answer").hide();
        $("#action-buttons > .mute").hide();
        $("#action-buttons > .hold").hide();
        $("#action-buttons > .unhold").hide();
        $("#action-buttons > .hangup").hide();
        $('div.agent-status').hide();
        $("#number-entry > input").val("");
    }

    SP.functions.setRingState = function () {
        $("#action-buttons > .answer").show();
        $("#action-buttons > .call").hide();
        $("#action-buttons > .mute").hide();
        $("#action-buttons > .hold").hide();
        $("#action-buttons > .unhold").hide();
        $("#action-buttons > .hangup").hide();
    }

    SP.functions.setOnCallState = function() {

        $("#action-buttons > .answer").hide();
        $("#action-buttons > .call").hide();
        $("#action-buttons > .mute").show();

        //can not hold outbound calls, so disable this
        if (SP.calltype == "Inbound") {
            $("#action-buttons > .hold").show();
        }

        $("#action-buttons > .hangup").show();
        $('div.agent-status').show();
    }
```

```
// Hide caller info
SP.functions.hideCallData = function() {
    $("#call-data").hide();
}
SP.functions.hideCallData();
SP.functions.setIdleState();

// Show caller info
SP.functions.showCallData = function(callData) {
    $("#call-data > ul").hide();
    $(".caller-name").text(callData.callerName);
    $(".caller-number").text(callData.callerNumber);
    $(".caller-queue").text(callData.callerQueue);
    $(".caller-message").text(callData.callerMessage);

    if (callData.callerName) {
        $("#call-data > ul.name").show();
    }

    if (callData.callerNumber) {
        $("#call-data > ul.phone_number").show();
    }

    if (callData.callerQueue) {
        $("#call-data > ul.queue").show();
    }

    if (callData.callerMessage) {
        $("#call-data > ul.message").show();
    }

    $("#call-data").slideDown(400);
}
```

```javascript
// Attach answer button to an incoming connection object
SP.functions.attachAnswerButton = function(conn) {
    $("#action-buttons > button.answer").
    click(function() {
    conn.accept();
    }).removeClass('inactive').addClass("active");
}

SP.functions.detachAnswerButton = function() {
    $("#action-buttons > button.answer").unbind().
    removeClass('active').addClass("inactive");
}

SP.functions.attachMuteButton = function(conn) {
    $("#action-buttons > button.mute").click(function() {
    conn.mute();
    SP.functions.attachUnMute(conn);
    }).removeClass('inactive').addClass("active").
    text("Mute");
}

SP.functions.attachUnMute = function(conn) {
    $("#action-buttons > button.mute").click(function() {
    conn.unmute();
    SP.functions.attachMuteButton(conn);
    }).removeClass('inactive').addClass("active").
    text("UnMute");
}

SP.functions.detachMuteButton = function() {
    $("#action-buttons > button.mute").unbind().
    removeClass('active').addClass("inactive");
}
```

```
SP.functions.attachHoldButton = function(conn) {
    $("#action-buttons > button.hold").click(function() {
      console.dir(conn);
      SP.requestedHold = true;
      //can't hold outbound calls from Twilio client
      $.post("/request_hold", { "from":SP.username,
      "callsid":conn.parameters.CallSid, "calltype":SP.
      calltype }, function(data) {
          //Todo: handle errors
          //Todo: change status in future
          SP.functions.attachUnHold(conn, data);

        });

    }).removeClass('inactive').addClass("active").
    text("Hold");
}

SP.functions.attachUnHold = function(conn, holdid) {
    $("#action-buttons > button.unhold").click(function() {
    //do ajax request to hold for the conn.id

      $.post("/request_unhold", { "from":SP.username,
      "callsid":holdid }, function(data) {
          //Todo: handle errors
          //Todo: change status in future
          //SP.functions.attachHoldButton(conn);
        });

    }).removeClass('inactive').addClass("active").
    text("UnHold").show();
}
```

```
SP.functions.detachHoldButtons = function() {
    $("#action-buttons > button.unhold").unbind().
    removeClass('active').addClass("inactive");
    $("#action-buttons > button.hold").unbind().
    removeClass('active').addClass("inactive");
}

SP.functions.updateAgentStatusText =
function(statusCategory, statusText, inboundCall) {

    if (statusCategory == "ready") {
        $("#agent-status-controls > button.ready").
        prop("disabled",true);
        $("#agent-status-controls > button.not-ready").
        prop("disabled",false);
        $("#agent-status").removeClass();
        $("#agent-status").addClass("ready");
        $('#softphone').removeClass('incoming');

    }

    if (statusCategory == "notReady") {
        $("#agent-status-controls > button.ready").
        prop("disabled",false);
        $("#agent-status-controls > button.not-ready").
        prop("disabled",true);
        $("#agent-status").removeClass();
        $("#agent-status").addClass("not-ready");
        $('#softphone').removeClass('incoming');
    }
```

```javascript
    if (statusCategory == "onCall") {
        $("#agent-status-controls > button.ready").
        prop("disabled",true);
        $("#agent-status-controls > button.not-ready").
        prop("disabled",true);
        $("#agent-status").removeClass();
        $("#agent-status").addClass("on-call");
        $('#softphone').removeClass('incoming');
    }

    if (inboundCall ==      true) {
    //alert("call from " + statusText);
    $('#softphone').addClass('incoming');
    $("#number-entry > input").val(statusText);
    }

    //$("#agent-status > p").text(statusText);
}

// Call button will make an outbound call (click to dial)
   to the number entered
$("#action-buttons > button.call").click( function( ) {
    params = {"PhoneNumber": $("#number-entry > input").
    val(), "CallerId": $("#callerid-entry > input").
    val()};
    Twilio.Device.connect(params);
});

// Hang up button will hang up any active calls
$("#action-buttons > button.hangup").click( function( ) {
    Twilio.Device.disconnectAll();
});
```

```
// Wire the ready / not ready buttons up to the server-
   side status change functions
$("#agent-status-controls > button.ready").click(
function( ) {
    $("#agent-status-controls > button.ready").
    prop("disabled",true);
    $("#agent-status-controls > button.not-ready").
    prop("disabled",false);
    SP.functions.ready();
});

$("#agent-status-controls > button.not-ready").click(
function( ) {
    $("#agent-status-controls > button.ready").prop
    ("disabled",false);
    $("#agent-status-controls > button.not-ready").
    prop("disabled",true);
    SP.functions.notReady();
});

$("#agent-status-controls > button.userinfo").click(
function( ) {
});

// ** Twilio Client Stuff ** //
// first register outside of sfdc

if ( window.self === window.top ) {
    console.log("Not in an iframe, assume we are using
    default client");
    var defaultclient = {}
    defaultclient.result = SP.username;
    SP.functions.registerTwilioClient(defaultclient);
```

```javascript
} else{
    console.log("In an iframe, assume it is Salesforce");
    sforce.interaction.isInConsole(SP.functions.
    getTwilioClientName);
}
//this will only be called inside of salesforce

Twilio.Device.ready(function (device) {
    sforce.interaction.cti.enableClickToDial();
    sforce.interaction.cti.onClickToDial(startCall);
    var adNag = function() {
        SP.functions.ready();
    };
    setTimeout(adNag, 1500);
});

Twilio.Device.offline(function (device) {
    //make a new status call.. something like..
    disconnected instead of notReady ?
    sforce.interaction.cti.disableClickToDial();
    SP.functions.notReady();
    SP.functions.hideCallData();
});

/* Report any errors on the screen */
Twilio.Device.error(function (error) {
    SP.functions.updateAgentStatusText("ready", error.
    message);
    SP.functions.hideCallData();
});
```

```
    /* Log a message when a call disconnects. */
    Twilio.Device.disconnect(function (conn) {
        console.log("disconnecting...");
        SP.functions.updateAgentStatusText("ready", "Call ended");

        SP.state.callNumber = null;

        // deactivate answer button
        SP.functions.detachAnswerButton();
        SP.functions.detachMuteButton();
        SP.functions.detachHoldButtons();
        SP.functions.setIdleState();

        SP.currentCall = null;

        // return to waiting state
        SP.functions.hideCallData();
        SP.functions.ready();
        //sforce.interaction.getPageInfo(saveLog);
    });

    Twilio.Device.connect(function (conn) {

        console.dir(conn);
        var     status = "";

        var callNum = null;
        if (conn.parameters.From) {
            callNum = conn.parameters.From;
            status = "Call From: " + callNum;
            SP.calltype = "Inbound";
        } else {
            status = "Outbound call";
            SP.calltype = "Outbound";

        }
```

```
console.dir(conn);

SP.functions.updateAgentStatusText("onCall", status);
SP.functions.setOnCallState();
SP.functions.detachAnswerButton();

SP.currentCall = conn;
SP.functions.attachMuteButton(conn);
SP.functions.attachHoldButton(conn, SP.calltype);

//send status info
SP.functions.update_agent(SP.username,{
    status: 'OnCall'
});
});

/* Listen for incoming connections */
Twilio.Device.incoming(function (conn) {
    // Update agent status
    sforce.interaction.setVisible(true);       //pop up CTI
                                                      console
    SP.functions.updateAgentStatusText("ready", ( conn.
    parameters.From), true);
    // Enable answer button and attach to incoming call
    SP.functions.attachAnswerButton(conn);
    SP.functions.setRingState();

    if (SP.requestedHold == true) {
        //auto answer
        SP.requestedHold = false;
        $("#action-buttons > button.answer").click();
    }
```

```
        var inboundnum = cleanInboundTwilioNumber(conn.
        parameters.From);
        var sid = conn.parameters.CallSid
        var result = "";
        //sfdc screenpop fields are specific to new contact
          screenpop
        sforce.interaction.searchAndScreenPop(inboundnum,
        'con10=' + inboundnum + '&con12=' + inboundnum +
        '&name_firstcon2=' + name,'inbound');

});


Twilio.Device.cancel(function(conn) {
        console.log(conn.parameters.From); // who canceled
                                            the call
        SP.functions.detachAnswerButton();
        SP.functions.detachHoldButtons();
        SP.functions.hideCallData();
        SP.functions.notReady();
        SP.functions.setIdleState();

        $(".number").unbind();
        SP.currentCall = null;
        //SP.functions.updateStatus();
});

$("#callerid-entry > input").change( function() {
        $.post("/setcallerid", { "from":SP.username,
        "callerid": $("#callerid-entry > input").val() });
});
```

```
// Set server-side status to ready / not-ready
SP.functions.notReady = function() {
    SP.functions.update_agent(SP.username,{
        status: 'NotReady'
    });
    SP.agentsRef.trigger('get-ready-agents',{username:
    SP.username});
    SP.functions.updateStatus();
}

SP.functions.ready = function() {
    SP.functions.update_agent(SP.username,{
        status: 'Ready'
    });
    SP.agentsRef.trigger('get-ready-agents',{username:
    SP.username});
    SP.functions.updateStatus();
}

// Check the status on the server and update the agent
   status dialog accordingly
SP.functions.updateStatus = function() {
    var data = SP.agent.status;
    if (data == "NotReady" || data == "Missed") {
        SP.functions.updateAgentStatusText("notReady",
        "Not Ready")
    }

    if (data == "Ready") {
        SP.functions.updateAgentStatusText("ready",
        "Ready")
    }
}
```

```
/******** GENERAL FUNCTIONS for SFDC    ****************/

function cleanInboundTwilioNumber(number) {
    //twilio inbound calls are passed with +1 (number).
      SFDC only stores
    return number.replace('+1','');
}

function cleanFormatting(number) {
    //changes a SFDC formatted US number, which would be
      415-555-1212
    return number.replace(' ','').replace('-','').
    replace('(','').replace(')','').replace('+','');
}

function startCall(response) {

    //called onClick2dial
    sforce.interaction.setVisible(true);      //pop up CTI
                                                     console
    var result = JSON.parse(response.result);
    var cleanedNumber = cleanFormatting(result.number);
    params = {"PhoneNumber": cleanedNumber, "CallerId":
    $("#callerid-entry > input").val()};
    Twilio.Device.connect(params);

}

var saveLogcallback = function (response) {
    if (response.result) {
        console.log("saveLog result =" + response.
        result);
```

```
    } else {
        console.log("saveLog error = " + response.
        error);
    }
};

function saveLog(response) {
    console.log("saving log result, response:");
    var result = JSON.parse(response.result);

    console.log(response.result);

    var timeStamp = new Date().toString();
    timeStamp = timeStamp.substring(0, timeStamp.
    lastIndexOf(':') + 3);
    var currentDate = new Date();
    var currentDay = currentDate.getDate();
    var currentMonth = currentDate.getMonth()+1;
    var currentYear = currentDate.getFullYear();
    var dueDate = currentYear + '-' + currentMonth +
    '-' + currentDay;
    var saveParams = 'Subject=' + SP.calltype +' Call
    on ' + timeStamp;

    saveParams += '&Status=completed';
    saveParams += '&CallType=' + SP.calltype;
    //should change this to reflect actual inbound or outbound
    saveParams += '&Activitydate=' + dueDate;
    saveParams += '&Phone=' + SP.state.callNumber;
    //we need to get this from.. somewhere
    saveParams += '&Description=' + "test description";

    console.log("About to parse    result..");
```

```
        var result = JSON.parse(response.result);
        var objectidsubstr = result.objectId.substr(0,3);
        // object id 00Q means a lead.. adding this to
           support logging on leads as well as contacts.
        if(objectidsubstr == '003' || objectidsubstr == '00Q') {
            saveParams += '&whoId=' + result.objectId;
        } else {
            saveParams += '&whatId=' + result.objectId;
        }

        console.log("save params = " + saveParams);
        sforce.interaction.saveLog('Task', saveParams,
        saveLogcallback);
    }
});
```

Once we set up our softphone, we make three AJAX calls to our backend:

1. /getconfig to return our Flybase info and enable our agentsRef and callsRef variables. Once agentsRef returns isReady from Flybase, then we trigger a call to our startWebSocket function. isReady is a function that we can use with the Flybase client when we wait to until our connection has been established before performing other actions.

2. /token to which we pass the agent's name and which returns a Twilio capability token to let the agent make and receive calls.

3. /getCallerId to return the outgoing phone number for the call to use.

We use the startWebSocket function (which was based on the original) to set up three event listeners and to update the agent's status as LogginIn and the time they came online.

Later in the Twilio Client code, we set the agent to Ready once their Twilio Client connection has been set up:

```
Twilio.Device.ready(function (device) {
    sforce.interaction.cti.enableClickToDial();
    sforce.interaction.cti.onClickToDial(startCall);
    var adNag = function() {
        SP.functions.ready();
    };
    setTimeout(adNag, 1500);
});
```

We are going to listen for agents-ready and in-queue events from our backend to tell the softphone to update the display to show the number of agents who are set to Ready and waiting for a call and then the number of callers who are in the queue waiting for an agent.

Finally, we're going to use the onDisconnect event to fire off an agent-removed trigger when the agent goes offline for some reason, such as closing the browser, logging off, etc.

You'll also notice a clone of our **update_agent** function in this file. One of the nice things about using Flybase is we can handle our database updates from either the frontend or the backend, so that lets us do a lot that we couldn't before.

The rest of the softphone.js file is actually the same as it was before. It talks to Twilio Client on incoming and outgoing calls, and it either gets the client name from the?client query string or it gets it from Salesforce, if you are displaying your softphone inside Salesforce.

You may also notice we make use of our new promises (http://blog.flybase.io/2016/02/02/promises-lookups/) functionality:

```
SP.functions.update_agent = function(client, data){
        var d = new Date();
        var date = d.toLocaleString();
        SP.agentsRef.where({"client": client}).once('value').
        then(function( rec ){
            var agent = rec.first().value();
            for( var i in data ){
                agent[i] = data[i];
            }
            SP.agent = agent;
            SP.agentsRef.push(agent, function(resp) {
                console.log( "agent updated" );
            });
        }, function(err){
            data.client = client;
            SP.agent = data;
            SP.agentsRef.push(data, function(resp) {
                console.log( "agent inserted" );
            });
        });
    }
SP.functions.update_agent = function(client, data){
        var d = new Date();
        var date = d.toLocaleString();
        SP.agentsRef.where({"client": client}).once('value').
        then(function( rec ){
            var agent = rec.first().value();
            for( var i in data ){
                agent[i] = data[i];
            }
```

```
        SP.agent = agent;
        SP.agentsRef.push(agent, function(resp) {
            console.log( "agent updated" );
        });
    }, function(err){
        data.client = client;
        SP.agent = data;
        SP.agentsRef.push(data, function(resp) {
            console.log( "agent inserted" );
        });
    });
}
```

In update_agent, we use promises to either return an existing agent record so we can update or create a brand-new record.

Deploying to Heroku (Optional)

This step is optional, and you can deploy anywhere you like.

You'll want a Heroku account and also to have the Heroku Toolbelt (https://toolbelt.heroku.com/) installed.

Create a file called "Profile" and include

```
web: node app.js
```

Now, run the following:

1. git init

2. heroku login to log into Heroku

3. heroku create to create the application within Heroku

4. `git add --all .` to add all of your new files to the repo

5. `git commit -am 'first commit'` to store the files inside the repo

6. `git push heroku master` to push your git repository to Heroku

7. `heroku open` to open your browser at your new, custom URL

The call center is now working. You can add `?client=ANYNAMEYOUWANT` to the end of the URL, and it will set you up as the agent.

Configuring Salesforce (Optional)

This step is optional. The call center works without Salesforce, and in part 2, we'll build a basic CRM that you can integrate this into as well.

This part is actually pretty simple. First, create a file called "TwilioAdapter.xml":

```xml
<?xml version="1.0" encoding="UTF-8" ?>
<callCenter>
  <section sortOrder="0" name="reqGeneralInfo" label="General
  Information">
    <item sortOrder="0" name="reqInternalName" label="Internal
    Name">DemoAdapter</item>
    <item sortOrder="1" name="reqDisplayName" label="Display
    Name">Demo Call Center Adapter</item>
    <item sortOrder="2" name="reqAdapterUrl" label="CTI Adapter
    URL">http://YOURWEBSITE.com</item>
    <item sortOrder="3" name="reqUseApi" label="Use CTI API">
    true</item>
```

```
    <item sortOrder="4" name="reqSoftphoneHeight"
    label="Softphone Height">400</item>
    <item sortOrder="5" name="reqSoftphoneWidth"
    label="Softphone Width">300</item>
  </section>
  <section sortOrder="1" name="reqDialingOptions"
  label="Dialing Options">
    <item sortOrder="0" name="reqOutsidePrefix" label="Outside
    Prefix">9</item>
    <item sortOrder="1" name="reqLongDistPrefix" label="Long
    Distance Prefix">1</item>
    <item sortOrder="2" name="reqInternationalPrefix"
    label="International Prefix">01</item>
  </section>
</callCenter>
```

Change the appropriate info to point to your website and then follow these steps:

1. Go to Call Centers ➤ Create:

   - Import a call center, config included,
   `TwilioAdapter.xml`. After import, change the
   parameter CTI Adapter URL to the Heroku
   URL created in the first steps: `https:/<insert`
   `yourherokuappurl.`

   - Add yourself to the call center under "Manage Call
   Center Users" ➤ Add More Users ➤ Find.

2. You should now see a CTI adapter under the
   Contact tab. However, you want to use the Service
   Cloud Console for all CTI calls (which prevents
   browser refreshes that would hang up calls).

3. To create a Service Cloud Console

    - Go to Setup ➤ Create ➤ Apps ➤ New.

    - Choose "Console" for the type of app.

    - Give it a name, such as "Twilio ACD."

    - Accept default for logo.

    - For tabs, add some tabs to your Service Cloud
      Console, such as Contacts, Cases, etc.

    - Accept default for step 5, "Choose how records
      display."

    - Set visibility to all (for dev orgs).

    - You've now created an app! You will see your
      console in the App dropdown, for example,
      "Twilio ACD."

4. Configure screenpops:

    - You can configure a screenpop response, such as
    to pop the search screen, in Setup ➤ Call Centers ➤
    (your call center) ➤ Softphone Layout.

These steps were borrowed from Charles' original post as they haven't changed.

Summary

Now you've got a working real-time call center ACD system that can be used stand-alone (as a lone softphone), in a CRM such as Salesforce, or in a CRM built entirely around it, which we'll do in part 2. If you're familiar at all with the original client-acd, then not much has changed, other than being rewritten in Node and using Flybase as the backend/signal system, and that was the plan with this chapter as I wanted to demonstrate how Flybase can be used within a call center, and this one has always been a go-to for various projects.

Just a reminder, you can find the full source code here: https://github.com/flybaseio/callcenter.

CHAPTER 6

Sending Daily SMS Reminders

In this chapter, I'll show you how you can use Node.js, Flybase, and Twilio to write your very own daily SMS reminder app.

Necessary Tools

- Twilio to send and receive SMS messages

- Flybase to store the users who have subscribed to our service

- Node.js to build on Chrome's JavaScript runtime for easily building fast, scalable network applications

Scheduling SMS Messages with Cron

To get started, we'll need to install a couple npm packages. We'll be using the twilio package (https://github.com/twilio/twilio-node) to send text messages, and we'll be using the cron package (https://github. com/ncb000gt/node-cron) to schedule the time we want to send the text messages. You can install them by running the following commands:

```
npm install twilio
npm install cron
```

© Roger Stringer 2021
R. Stringer, *Real-Time Twilio and Flybase*, https://doi.org/10.1007/978-1-4842-7074-5_6

Create a new file called app.js and require the twilio and cron packages:

```
var twilio = require('twilio'),
client = twilio('ACCOUNTSID', 'AUTHTOKEN'),
cronJob = require('cron').CronJob;
```

Let's write some code that sends a text message at 6 PM every day:

```
var textJob = new cronJob( '0 18 * * *', function(){
  client.sendMessage( { to:'YOURPHONENUMBER',
  from:'YOURTWILIONUMBER', body:'Hello! Hope you're having a
  good day!' }, function( err, data ) {});
}, null, true);
```

You're probably wondering what the string we're passing as the first argument to our cronJob is. That is a format specific to Cron that lets us define the time and frequency of when we want this job to fire.

In this case, at 0 minutes 18 hours every day. This article (`www.nncron.ru/help/EN/working/cron-format.htm`) does a nice job of breaking down the Cron format.

In the callback to our cronJob, we use the Twilio Client library to send a message. We pass the to and from numbers and the body of the message we want to send.

Run this code and wait in anticipation for your text message. If it's 10 AM, you probably don't want to have to wait 8 hours to see if your code works. Just update the Cron format to send at an earlier time. Here's a hint. To send at 10:13 AM, you'd use this format: "13 10 * * *".

You now have a basic version of this app, but you most likely don't want to just send a message to yourself every day. If you do, then congrats! You're all done! For the rest of us, we can make a couple small code changes to have this send to multiple phone numbers.

First, let's add a new variable called numbers that contains the phone numbers we want to send messages to:

```
var numbers = ['YOURPHONENUMBER', 'YOURFRIENDSPHONENUMBER'];
```

Then let's update the code in our textJob to loop over these phone numbers and send a message to them:

```
for( var i = 0; i &lt; numbers.length; i++ ) {
  client.sendMessage( { to:numbers[i], from:'YOURTWILIONUMBER',
  body:'Hello! Hope you're having a good day.'}, function( err,
  data ) {
    console.log( data.body );
  });
}
```

Receiving SMS Messages

Now that we're sending an SMS message to different numbers at our desired time, let's update this code to know when a user sends a text message to our app. Twilio uses webhooks (https://en.wikipedia.org/wiki/Webhook) to let your server know when an incoming message or phone call comes into our app. We need to set up an endpoint that we can tell Twilio to use for the messaging webhook.

We'll be using the Express framework (http://expressjs.com/) to set up our node web server to receive the POST request from Twilio, so we'll need to install the express package. We'll also be using the body-parser module, so we're going to install that as well:

npm install express
npm install body-parser

At the beginning of our app.js file, we'll need to require express and initialize it into a variable called app. We're also going to use the bodyParser middleware (https://github.com/expressjs/body-parser) to make it easy to use the data we'll get in our POST request:

```
var express = require('express'),
bodyParser = require('body-parser'),
app = express();
app.use(bodyParser.json());
app.use(bodyParser.urlencoded({
  extended: true
}));
```

We're going to add a route for /message that responds with some TwiML (www.twilio.com/docs/api/twiml). TwiML is a basic set of instructions you can use to tell Twilio what to do when you receive an incoming call or SMS message. Our code will look like this:

```
app.post('/message', function (req, res) {
  var resp = new twilio.TwimlResponse();
  resp.message('Thanks for subscribing!');
  res.writeHead(200, {
    'Content-Type':'text/xml'
  });
  res.end(resp.toString());
});
```

We use the Twilio node library to initialize a new TwimlResponse. We then use the Message verb (www.twilio.com/docs/api/twiml/sms/message) to set what we want to respond to the message with. In this case, we'll just say "Thanks for subscribing!" Then we'll set the content-type of our response to text/xml and send the string representation of the TwimlResponse we built.

Finally, let's set our server to listen on port 3000:

```
var server = app.listen(3000, function() {
  console.log('Listening on port %d', server.address().port);
});
```

Now let's fire up our app:

node app.js

Now that we have our server running, we need to tell Twilio to use this messaging URL as our Message Request URL:

![](https://lh6.googleusercontent.com/EDpe7a4_
f17kekwXJmzaPj53kvW913UZHr-lEvlKP588mR5jHzIzUd7g48GSzkSzz5INNI9
sh3Mygtmstiz4YmCuFznnTSlWpZVObEFXjjnlU8mZzHR_SL-7nyEHWTmolw)

Send an SMS message to your Twilio number, and you should get a response back. If you don't, take a look at the Twilio App Monitor (`www.twilio.com/user/account/developer-tools/app-monitor`) to help determine what went wrong.

Saving Users in Flybase

We've set up a script that sends out a text message at the same time every day, and we've given users the ability to send a text message into our app. There's just one last thing left to do. We need to save our users' information when they send a text to our app. We'll be using Flybase (`www.flybase.io/`) as our datastore, so we need to install the Flybase node module:

npm install flybase

Now that we've installed the Flybase module, let's require and initialize it at the top of our app.js file:

```
var api_key = "{YOUR-API-KEY}";
var db = "dailysms";
var collection = "users";

var usersRef = require('flybase').init(db, collection, api_key);
```

When you sign for a Flybase account, they provide an API Key for your account. Make sure you update this code to replace {YOUR-API-KEY} with this key.

From inside Flybase, create a new app called dailysms.

Since we'll be pulling the phone numbers from Flybase, we'll want to update our numbers variable to be an empty array and then fill it with info from the database.

Flybase is a real-time database and built around the premise of subscribing to events as opposed to reading on demand. We're going to subscribe to two events: first, we want to retrieve a list of all existing phone numbers, and then we want to get notified whenever a new user is added:

```
var numbers = [];
usersRef.on('value', function(snapshot) {
        snapshot.forEach( function( rec ){
                numbers.push( rec.value().phonenumber );
                console.log( 'Added number ' + rec.value().
                phonenumber );
        });
});

usersRef.on('added', function(snapshot) {
        numbers.push( snapshot.value().phonenumber );
        console.log( 'Added number ' + snapshot.value().
        phonenumber );
});
```

Now we need to add users to our database when they text in subscribe. Let's revisit our message route to make this update:

```javascript
app.post('/message', function (req, res) {
    var resp = new twilio.TwimlResponse();
    if( req.body.Body.trim().toLowerCase() === 'subscribe' ) {
        var fromNum = req.body.From;
        if(numbers.indexOf(fromNum) !== -1) {
            resp.message('You already subscribed!');
        } else {
            resp.message('Thank you, you are now subscribed.
            Reply "STOP" to stop receiving updates.');
            usersRef.push({phonenumber:fromNum});
        }
    } else {
        resp.message('Welcome to Daily Updates. Text
        "Subscribe" receive updates.');
    }
    res.writeHead(200, {
        'Content-Type':'text/xml'
    });
    res.end(resp.toString());
});
```

When the Twilio message webhook triggers a new POST request to your server, we include request parameters (www.twilio.com/docs/api/twiml/sms/twilio_request#request-parameters) with information about the message.

We'll be using the Body parameter to examine the content the user texted in and the From parameter to determine the number they texted from. If they've texted in the word "subscribe" and they're not already in our database, we'll use the push function on our Flybase reference to add them.

Our app is now ready to go. Let's run it and give it a try:

```
node app.js
```

Summary

We did it! Now that you've built a simple daily SMS reminder app, it's your chance to customize the daily message to whatever you want.

CHAPTER 7

Building a Real-Time Call Tracking Dashboard

This chapter will show you how to implement a real-time call tracking dashboard.

We'll do this in two parts: the first part will be a simple Node.js file that accepts incoming calls from Twilio and then stores the information inside a Flybase app, and the second part is the dashboard itself.

We're going to display two stats, the incoming Twilio phone number and the city the call originated from. You can build on this further later.

With our original dashboard, we passed events and didn't actually store any information. This time we'll be storing the information to retrieve later.

The Backend

Let's build the backend section of your dashboard.

First, let's set up our "package.json" file:

```
{
  "name": "call-tracking",
  "version": "1.0.0",
```

```
  "description": "Example app demonstrating how to do call
                  tracking with Twilio and Flybase",
  "main": "index.js",
  "scripts": {
    "test": "echo \"Error: no test specified\" && exit 1"
  },
  "repository": {
    "type": "git",
    "url": "git+https://github.com/flybaseio/call-tracking.git"
  },
  "author": "",
  "license": "ISC",
  "bugs": {
    "url": "https://github.com/flybaseio/call-tracking/issues"
  },
  "homepage": "https://github.com/flybaseio/call-
                tracking#readme",
  "dependencies": {
    "body-parser": "^1.15.2",
    "compression": "^1.6.2",
    "cors": "^2.8.1",
    "ejs": "^2.5.2",
    "express": "^4.14.0",
    "flybase": "^1.7.8",
    "method-override": "^2.3.6",
    "serve-static": "^1.11.1"
  }
}
```

Now, let's set up our "index.js" file to run as our backend:

```javascript
var http = require('http');
var express = require('express');
var bodyParser = require('body-parser');
var flybase = require('flybase');
var path = require('path');

var cors = require('cors');
var compression = require('compression');
var serveStatic = require('serve-static');

var app = express();
app.set('view engine', 'ejs');
app.use(bodyParser.json());
app.use(bodyParser.urlencoded({    extended: true    }));
app.use(express.static( path.join(__dirname, 'public')));

var port = process.env.PORT || 5000; // set our port

var flybaseRef = flybase.init('YOUR-FLYBASE-APP-NAME',
                "calltracking", 'YOUR-FLYBASE-API-KEY');

//      backend

app.post('/call', function(req, res) {
    flybaseRef.push({
        time: Date.now()/1000,
        number: req.body.To,
        city: req.body.FromCity
    }).then( function( rec ){
        res.type('text/xml');
        res.render('twiml', { message: 'Your call has been
        recorded!' })
    }, function(err){
```

```javascript
        res.type('text/xml');
        console.log(error);
        res.render('twiml', { message: 'Sorry, an error
        happened.' });
    });
});
```

Now, let's add the frontend handler. This will just be part of the same "index.js" file:

```javascript
// frontend

function setCustomCacheControl(res, path) {
    if (serveStatic.mime.lookup(path) === 'text/html') {
        // Custom Cache-Control for HTML files
        res.setHeader('Cache-Control', 'public, max-age=0')
    }
}

app.use(compression());

app.use(serveStatic(__dirname + '/dashboard', {
    maxAge: '1d',
    setHeaders: setCustomCacheControl,
    'index': ['index.html'],
    fallthrough: true
}));

var server = http.createServer(app);
server.listen(process.env.PORT || 3000, function() {
    console.log('Express server started.');
});
```

I'm using the **serve-static** module here since the dashboard can be stand-alone if we want it to be, so it's just your standard HTML page served statically, so we'll tell our app to display any file inside the dashboard folder.

Finally, we need to create a folder called views and add a tiny little file called twiml.ejs:

```
<Response>
    <Say><%= message %></Say>
</Response>
```

This is used to return our TwiML (Twilio Markup Language) response on incoming calls. You can play with this further to make it do things like connect a call to another number and so on, but for this app, we just need to record and track.

The Frontend

We want this dashboard to be able to run anywhere, so we're just going to include the dashboard folder and set up our Node app to serve it statically. You can actually upload the dashboard folder anywhere you want and have it run and display your call tracking stats.

Create a folder called dashboard. Now, create a file inside the dashboard folder called index.html:

```
<!doctype html>
<html>
    <head>
        <title>Call Tracking On the Fly</title>
```

```
            <link href="https://maxcdn.bootstrapcdn.
            com/bootstrap/3.3.6/css/bootstrap.min.css"
            rel="stylesheet" integrity="sha256-7s5uDGW3A
            Hqw6xtJmNNtr+OBRJUlgkNJEo78P4bOyRw= sha512-
            nNo+yCHEynOsmMxSswnf/OnX6/KwJuZTlNZBjauKhTKOc
            +zT+q5JOCxOUFhXQ6rJR9jg6Es8gPuD2uZcYDLqSw=="
            crossorigin="anonymous">
            <link href="https://cdnjs.cloudflare.com/ajax/libs/
            epoch/0.5.2/epoch.min.css" rel="stylesheet" />
            <link href="dashboard.css" rel="stylesheet" />
    </head>
    <body>
            <div class="navbar-nav navbar-inverse navbar-fixed-top">
                    <div class="container">
                    <div class="navbar-header">
                            <button type="button" class="navbar-
                            toggle" data-toggle="collapse" data-
                            target=".navbar-collapse">
                                    <span class="icon-bar"></span>
                                    <span class="icon-bar"></span>
                                    <span class="icon-bar"></span>
                            </button>
                            <a class="navbar-brand" href="index.
                            html">
                                    Call Tracking Dashboard
                            </a>
                    </div>
                            <div class="navbar-collapse collapse">
                                    <ul class="nav navbar-nav">
                                            <li class="active">
```

```
                        <!-- <a href="index.
                        html">
                                <i class="icon-
                                home icon-
                                white"></i> Home
                        </a> -->
                    </li>
                </ul>
            </div><!--/.nav-collapse -->
        </div>
    </div>

    <div class="container">

        <div class="row">

            <div class="col-sm-12 col-lg-12">
                <article class="widget">
                    <div class="widget-inner">

                        <header>
                            <h1>Calls</h1>
                        </header>

                        <section class="widget-
                        body">
                            <div id="calls"
                            class="epoch"
                            style="height:
                            200px;"></div>
                        </section>

                    </div><!-- .widget-inner -->
```

```
                    </article>
            </div>

        </div>

        <div class="row">

            <div class="col-sm-6 col-lg-6">
                <article class="widget">
                    <div class="widget-inner">

                        <header>
                            <h1>Incoming Number</h1>
                        </header>

                        <section class="widget-body">
                            <div id="numbers"
                            class="epoch"
                            style="height:
                            200px;"></div>
                        </section>

                    </div><!-- .widget-inner -->

                </article>
            </div>

            <div class="col-sm-6 col-lg-6">
                <article class="widget">
                    <div class="widget-inner">

                        <header>
                            <h1>City</h1>
                        </header>
```

```html
                    <section class="widget-
                    body">
                            <div id="cities"
                            class="epoch"
                            style="height:
                            200px;"></div>
                    </section>

            </div><!-- .widget-inner -->

        </article>
      </div>
    </div>

  </div>

<script src="https://cdnjs.cloudflare.com/ajax/libs/
jquery/2.1.4/jquery.min.js"></script>
<script src="https://cdnjs.cloudflare.com/ajax/libs/
d3/3.5.10/d3.min.js"></script>
<script src="https://cdnjs.cloudflare.com/ajax/libs/
epoch/0.5.2/epoch.min.js"></script>
<script src="https://cdn.flybase.io/flybase.js"></script>
<script src="dashboard.js"></script>
</body>
</html>
```

You will next create a file called dashboard.js:

```javascript
$( function() {
    var calls = $('#calls').epoch( {
        type: 'time.area', axes: ['left', 'bottom', 'right'],
        data: [ { values: [ { time: Date.now()/1000, y: 0 } ] } ]
    } );
```

149

```
var numbers = $( '#numbers' ).epoch( { type: 'bar' } );
var cities = $( '#cities' ).epoch( { type: 'bar' } );
var stats = {
     cities: {},
     numbers: {}
};

var dashboard = new Flybase("YOUR-FLYBASE-API-KEY",
"calltracking", "stats");

dashboard.once('value', function (data) {
     updateStats( data );
});

dashboard.on( 'added', function (data ){
     updateStats( data );
});

function updateStats( data ){
     //       process the new data...
     data.forEach( function( snapshot ){
          var row = snapshot.value();

          calls.push( [ { time: row.time, y: 1 } ] );

          var cityCount = stats.cities[ row.city ] || 0;
          stats.cities[ row.city ] = ++cityCount;

          var numberCount = stats.numbers[ row.number ] || 0;
          stats.numbers[ row.number ] = ++numberCount;
     });

     var citiesData = [];
     for( var city in stats.cities ) {
```

```
            citiesData.push( { x: city, y: stats.cities[
            city ] } );
        }
        cities.update( [ { values: citiesData } ] );

        var numbersData = [];
        for( var number in stats.numbers ) {
            numbersData.push( { x: number, y: stats.numbers[
            number ] } );
        }
        numbers.update( [ { values: numbersData } ] );

    }
});
```

This is the brains of our dashboard; it processes all calls and displays them in the dashboard.

Finally, let's add some CSS.

Create a file called "dashboard.css" and add the following:

```
body {
  font: 400 0.95em/1 "Proxima Nova", Helvetica,sans-serif;
  font-size: .875em;
  background-color: #f0f0f0;

  padding-top: 90px;
}

.widget {
  -webkit-box-shadow: #f0f0f0 0 0 8px;
  -moz-box-shadow: #f0f0f0 0 0 8px;
  box-shadow: #f0f0f0 0 0 8px;
  background-color: #f0f0f0;

  margin-bottom: 30px;
}
```

```
.widget h1 {
  font-size: 1.0em;
  margin: 0 0 .4em;
  font-weight: bold;
}

.widget .widget-inner>header, .widget .widget-inner>footer {
  font-size: 12px;
  text-shadow: 1px 1px #0e0e0e;
}

.widget .widget-inner>header {
  background-color: #272727;
  text-transform: uppercase;
  padding: 16px 12px 16px 26px;
  font-weight: 700;
}

.widget .widget-inner {
  border: solid 1px #e5e5e5;
  background-color: #fff;
}

.widget .widget-inner>header {
  background-color: #f5f5f5;
}

.widget .widget-inner>header h1 {
  color: #8b8b8b;
  text-shadow: 1px 1px #fff;
  margin-bottom: 0;
}
```

```css
.widget .widget-body {
  color: #666;

  height: 225px
}

.widget .widget-body {
  padding: 16px;
  color: #d3d4d4;
  font-family: Helvetica, Arial, sans-serif;
  z-index: 1;
}

.widget .widget-inner>footer {
  color: #8b8b8b;
  background-color: #f5f5f5;
  text-shadow: 1px 1px #fff;
}

.dash-unit {
  margin-bottom: 30px;
  padding-bottom: 10px;
  border: 1px solid #e5e5e5;
  /*background-image: url('../img/sep-half.png');*/
  background-color: #f5f5f5;
  color: #8b8b8b;
  height: 290px;
  text-align: center;
}

.dash-unit dtitle {
  font-size: 11px;
  text-transform: uppercase;
  margin: 8px;
```

```
  padding: 0px;
  height: inherit;
}

.dash-unit hr {
  border: 0;
  border-top: 1px solid #151515;
  border-top-style: dashed;
  margin-top: 3px;
}
```

Summary

You can run this anywhere you want. You just have to point your Twilio phone number(s) you want to track to the URL you add to this site with /call as the endpoint. You can see the full codebase at GitHub: https://github.com/flybaseio/call-tracking.

Index

© Roger Stringer 2021
R. Stringer, *Real-Time Twilio and Flybase*, https://doi.org/10.1007/978-1-4842-7074-5

Printed in the United States
by Baker & Taylor Publisher Services

Printed in the United States
by Baker & Taylor Publisher Services